W9-AXO-666

KITES
AND OTHER WIND MACHINES

ANDRE THIEBAULT

 Sterling Publishing Co., Inc. New York

Translated and adapted by Louisa Bumagin Hellegers.

Drawings by Bruno Le Sourd.

Photographs by Monique Lafon.

Pages 74 to 79 were contributed by Albert Boekholt.

Library of Congress Cataloging in Publication Data

Thiebault, Andre.
   Kites, and other wind machines.

   Translation of: Cerfs-volants.
   Includes index.
   I. Kites.   I. Hellegers, Louisa Bumagin.
II. Le Sourd, Bruno.   III. Lafon, Monique.
IV. Title.
TL759.T4713   1982   629.133′32   82-50554
ISBN 0-8069-5464-7
ISBN 0-8069-5465-5 (lib. bdg.)

Copyright © 1982 by Sterling Publishing Co., Inc.
Two Park Avenue, New York, N.Y. 10016
Originally published in France under the title "cerfs-volants"
Copyright © 1978 by Editions du Centurion
Distributed in Australia by Oak Tree Press Co., Ltd.
P.O. Box K514 Haymarket, Sydney 2000, N.S.W.
Distributed in the United Kingdom by Blandford Press
Link House, West Street, Poole, Dorset BH15 1LL, England
Distributed in Canada by Oak Tree Press Ltd.
% Canadian Manda Group, 215 Lakeshore Boulevard East
Toronto, Ontario M5A 3W9
Manufactured in the United States of America
All rights reserved
Library of Congress Catalog Card No.: 82-50554
Sterling ISBN 0-8069-5464-7 Trade
                  -5465-5 Library

Contents

USES OF KITES

Introduction

Techniques related to kite-making are as important as flinging the kite into the air; therefore, this guidebook will enable you to learn and develop such skills. We are less concerned with teaching you the actual techniques for making kites than with ensuring the fun you can have and the education you can gain from such a creative activity. Kite-making is particularly enjoyable because it appeals equally to boys and girls—no matter what their ages! In addition, there is an infinite variety of possible models you can make using the patterns shown in this book. You can begin with a simple sheet of cutout notebook paper and make a kite that is ready to fly in five minutes!

A brief history of kites can help acquaint you with kite-making. Kite-flying was not always a simple children's game; indeed, it was not in that form that kites originated.

The names given to kites in various countries support the theory that kites may have been invented in the Far East. For example, in Germany, Denmark, Scotland and the Soviet Union, the kite is known by the name "dragon." It is well known that the Chinese frequently make their kites in the shape of a dragon. In England and the United States, the name "kite" is used; this word resembles the meaning of the Cambodian word *kléng*.

In Cambodia, there is a story that is told about the kite, which is as follows:

A long time ago, a king reigned in China who was not affectionate towards the Khmer people. One day he imprisoned one of them—Thmenh Cei. Because he wished to escape, Thmenh Cei set out to win the sympathy of one of his jailors. Thanks to the jailor, Thmenh Cei was able to pass a message to a young Cambodian boy he knew to be very creative. Then he waited, full of confidence.

Without losing an instant, the young boy set to work. He made a large *kléng* (kite), and when it was almost finished, he completed it with an *ék*, a sort of arch that held a network of very thin bamboo. On a very dark night when the wind made the palace doors rattle, the king was awakened by a strange noise. It was a sort of vibration which arose, built up, diminished and then disappeared. One could have said that a lament was heard that seemed to come from the sky.

The king, who was far from having a tranquil conscience, had frightful nightmares.

And the following night, the strange noise began again!

It was obvious that the spirits of the night personally wanted the king. Urgent protective measures were imposed, and the most qualified monks were summoned. They consulted at length and finally unanimously decreed that the ghastly noise the king heard was an intervention of the Bird of Misfortune. It seemed to them that the only way to appease the Bird was to liberate the prisoner (Thmenh Cei), and the king agreed, not knowing that it was a kite which had made all that frightful noise he had heard.

The king thought it wise to show great consideration for Thmenh Cei and showered him with many gifts so that Thmenh Cei could only consider his detention as a pleasant and momentary respite from the bother and routine of his daily life.

Kites and the Spirits

Probably one of the main reasons for the existence of kites in certain areas was the belief that kites could help one deal with the spirits. In the Far East, kites served to attract the attention of the spirits to whom it was good to address one's prayers. There, kites were given the shapes of dragons, fish, or some other fantastic beings, the particular form depending upon the nature and temperament of the intended character. For effectiveness, the kites were provided with whistles or harps which shook with the wind. Some rectangular or cylindrical kites contained candles to transform them into flying lanterns, to ensure that they did not fly past the spirits unnoticed.

In Cambodia, at the full moon of *maskir* (November), the king and his subjects flew huge *kléng-phongs* (ritual kites about 3 or 4 yards [3 or 4 metres] long) in the middle of the night. During this time, the monks prayed psalms over the flight area (see Fig. 1).

Little by little, these Cambodian rituals disappeared until the end of the last century, when one could once again see monks solemnly flying their kites above their pagodas to turn away the evil spirits. In Korea, during the first 15 days of the year, people wrote on their kites the names and birth dates of those children they wished to shelter from the turmoils of the spirits. When the kites were flying sufficiently high, they loosened them completely, so that the wind would take them as far away as possible, thus leading away the evil spirits that pursued them.

Today, the kite is again part of many festivals (the Vietnamese festival of Tet, for example), but kites have lost their religious meaning; they are usually now flown by children.

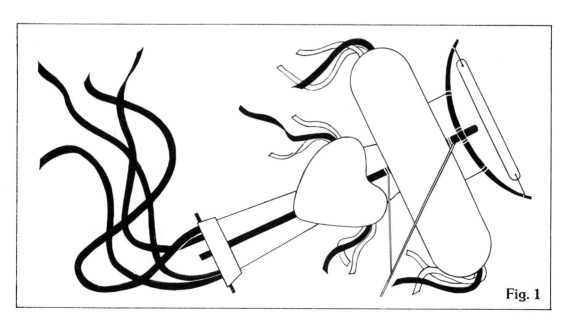

Fig. 1

Military Kites

In the year 206 B.C., Chinese General Han-Sin besieged a city. Because the city's resistance lasted longer than pleased Han-Sin, he decided to dig out a tunnel which would lead into the heart of the area. He had the idea of calculating the distance he needed to cover by flying a kite over the chosen destination.

In 1689 in Siam, the king of Ayuthya reconquered his capital by unfurling kites loaded with explosives over the capital.

In England in 1894, Lieutenant Robert Baden-Powell conceived of replacing a crowded hilltop observation tower with an easily transportable kite. His first device was 11 yards (11 metres) long. It was steered by two cables which supported a cockpit that did not take off until the kite was in the air. Under the cockpit hung the cables that his aides held on to from the ground in order to ensure that the cockpit did not swing.

The following year, Lt. Baden-Powell gave his invention more security by harnessing several slightly smaller kites, one behind the other (see Fig. 2).

In 1897 in the United States, a Lieutenant Wise raised up two trains of kites attached to a single cable from which hung a pulley (see Fig. 3). This pulley allowed a swing (in which the observer sat) to be hoisted and rapidly lowered in case of danger.

Similar experiments were conducted in various other areas in the world. For instance, several years before the First World War, French Captain Sacconey created and trained entire platoons to fly kites; the overwhelming development of aviation, however, made their use obsolete.

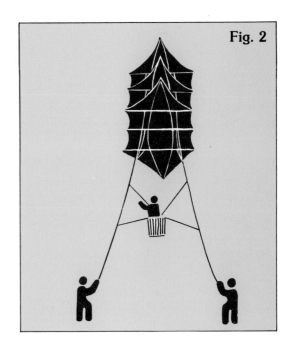

Fig. 2

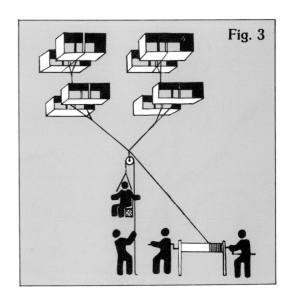

Fig. 3

Postal Kites

In the year 549, a city in China was besieged. Feeling that his troops were ready to change camps, the very honorable General in command had the idea to draft some urgent messages demanding that relief columns be immediately sent. He attached the messages to kites, which he unfurled in all directions. The aerial post was invented!

In 1897, American Lieutenant Wise devoted himself to experimenting with signal systems which utilized kites. The use of three differently colored devices permitted him to establish a code with which to communicate. He also used colored lanterns and flags hoisted by means of ropes which he directed from the ground.

the dangerous experimentation with kites that has taken place.

Writers at the end of the eighteenth century wrote of a woman who had succeeded in leaving the ground by means of a kite.

In December 1856, on the beach of Sainte-Anne-La-Palud in France, a sailor, Jean Le Bris, raised himself into the air with the help of a kite attached to the back of a cart pulled by a galloping horse.

In 1868, Biot attempted an ascension with the use of kites that was crowned a success. Then, Maillot, who did not chance leaving the ground himself, raised up sacks of impressive weight by using increasingly larger and heavier kites. His last model was an octagon weighing 442 pounds (210 kg). He manoeuvred it from the ground with two cords which controlled the "aviator in the cockpit" (sack). Other lines, as shown in Fig. 4, were manned by people on the ground to ensure that the experiment didn't fly away!

Kites and Their Ascents

The story exists of an all-powerful mandarin who one day devised a means by which he thought he could visit the spirits in their own realm. He attached a group of kites to an armchair into which he positioned himself, but the armchair did not fly up. He then decided to facilitate his takeoff by foolishly tying enormous firecrackers to the feet of his armchair. After lighting the firecrackers, an explosion ensued, killing the mandarin. This is but one example of

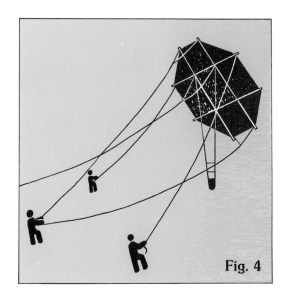

Fig. 4

Kites and Science

In 1752, Benjamin Franklin captured electricity from the clouds by using a kite. Many scholars later used the kite to erect barometers, thermometers, hygrometers (to measure humidity) and anemometers (to measure wind pressure or velocity). It seems that the first attempts at these constructions took place in 1877.

Kites and Hunting

The Chinese had the idea of attaching whistles to their kites to cause game to flock together. Having heard of this, some Parisians made kites in the form of sparrow hawks whose mission (as told to the newspapers of 1897) was to frighten partridges to death, making hunting for these birds much easier.

Kites and Photography

It was in France in 1888 that Arthur Battut had the idea of using a kite to take aerial photographs, either for use in topographical studies or for observing areas to which it was difficult to obtain access. Numerous arrangements of the equipment were studied; the mechanism for the taking of the pictures was either attached directly to the kite or was hoisted along the flying line by means of a second kite or a pulley. The shutter was set in motion either by a fuse which burned itself up slowly, by a string set up especially to control and perform the task from the ground, or by an automatic-timer mechanism.

Kites and Fishing

Apparently, long ago, certain people from the Pacific islands used kites to fish in the open sea, while remaining on the shore themselves. Our studies have, unfortunately, not yet explained the methods that were used.

Kites and Rescues

Several inventions using kites were used in rescue missions.

In 1892, an American, Woodbridge Davis, completed a kite that towed a mooring rope. It was about 2 yards (2 metres) in diameter and was covered with oiled sailcloth to resist the fog. From a certain distance, two manoeuvring cables allowed the kite to be directed towards a ship in distress. When the kite was in the desired direction, it was attached to a lifesaver to which a rope was secured to help direct the rescue (see Fig. 5).

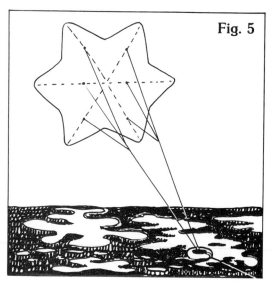

Fig. 5

Fig. 6

Kites and Freight

It seems natural that someone would try to use the kite as a means of pulling. Many experiments and numerous projects were carried out to this end.

The polar expedition of Captain Austin in 1850 utilized kites to haul sleds across the ice fields. In 1890, an American applied for a patent for a train of transatlantic kites. This train supported a cockpit for passengers and was lashed to a heavy raft which offered the necessary resistance for the kites (see Fig. 6). If this experiment had no following, it is probably because the prospective passengers never had the courage to embark!

Kites and Art

In the Far East, the kite is valued not only for its technical qualities, but also for its original shapes and artistic decorations.

Since the thirteenth century, the Siamese (Thais) have come to the king's court to exhibit their beautiful kites and to receive congratulations and beg for certain privileges. Fig. 7 on page 15 shows examples of these kites.

Kites and Sports

At the end of the last century, kites were very much in vogue, and kite tournaments were held in the United States. There were also contests of height; one kite apparently flew for three hours at an altitude of 15,000 feet (5,000 metres).

Since 1906, kite-flying contests have become a national sport in Thailand. The season for the meets is between February and April, and the king himself comes to present the awards.

The contest area is divided in two by a stretched cord. Several *papkaos*—"female" kites that measure about 30 inches (75 cm)—are thrown on one side of the cord. Their tail is comprised of a long ribbon which is supposed to be wrapped around the opponent kite to throw it off balance.

An entire team creates the *chula*—the male kite—on the other half of the playing area. The chula measures 2 yards (2 metres), sometimes more. The intent of the male kite is to demolish the *papkaos* and to lead them back to their own camp.

Another sport we can mention here is water-skiing with kites. The first championships in this field took place in Vichy, France, in 1963. The flying delta wing or delta plane can be considered as much a kite as a glider. The first championships took place in South Africa.

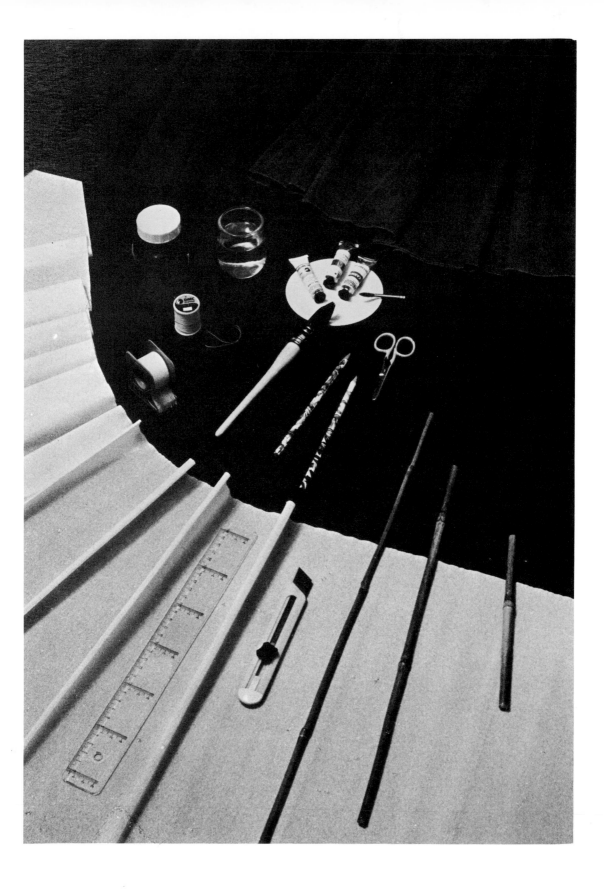

KITE CONSTRUCTION

Equipment for the Workshop

Equipment

- Yard or metre stick for measuring
- Pocketknife
- Scissors
- Paintbrush for glue

Basic Material

This depends on the type of kite you wish to make.

Material for the Framework

- Straw broom that you can take apart and then use the pieces for the foundation stakes.
- Caning or a flower basket from which you can salvage the thin straw strips.
- Bamboo, which is more resistant than cane, but is also somewhat heavier.
- Very straight sticks made from tree branches can be used in place of the bamboo. Weight the sticks down at the ends and let them dry out in the shade.
- Rattan about ⅛ inch (3 to 3.5 mm) in diameter for certain supports for Oriental kites.
- Linen thread to outline the border of the kites and to make the bindings.
- Adhesive tape to join certain parts.
- Metal pins to attach or temporarily hold the supports in place.

Material for the Sail

- Notebook paper to make small, simple models.
- Newspaper for slightly larger models.
- Colored poster paper.
- Kraft (brown) wrapping paper, which is stronger than poster paper and is good to use for larger models.
- Tissue paper, colored crepe paper or rice paper, which is strong, lightweight and particularly good to use to make pocketed kites.
- Powdered glue.
- Quick-drying white glue.
- Various, fairly lightweight fabrics.
- Sewing equipment.

Material for the Cables

- Sewing thread strong enough to secure the frames for small models.
- Linen thread to use for light winds with kites that measure no more than 24 inches (60 cm) in length.
- Hemp rope for larger models.
- Strong nylon fishing line for very large kites.

Fig. 7

Some Don'ts

Never launch a kite near an electrical wire, and never fly a kite over such a high wire. If the kite descends unexpectedly onto the wire, it can transmit a fatal electrical charge, especially in damp or humid weather. It is just as dangerous to fly a kite during a storm.

Practical and General Advice

A kite must have three qualities: lightness, resistance and rigidity of all or part of the frame, which depend on your choice of frames, connections and sails (see Fig. 8).

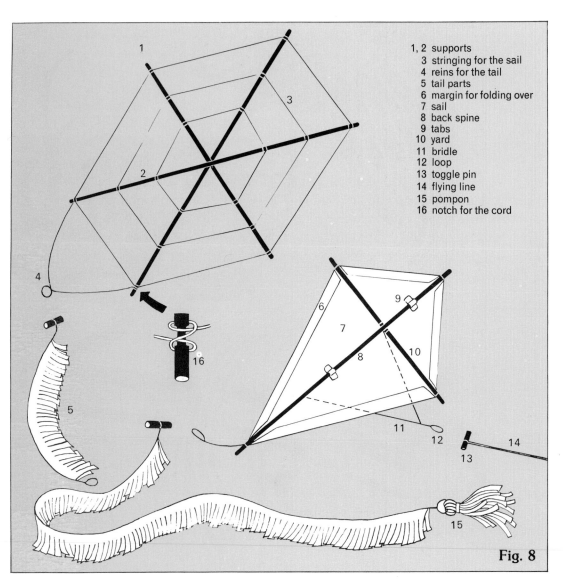

1, 2 supports
3 stringing for the sail
4 reins for the tail
5 tail parts
6 margin for folding over
7 sail
8 back spine
9 tabs
10 yard
11 bridle
12 loop
13 toggle pin
14 flying line
15 pompon
16 notch for the cord

Fig. 8

The Framework

The framework, which must be as light as possible, consists of the supports and a rope. The resistance it offers to the wind must be proportionate to the size of the kite.

The "wings"—that is, the two opposite sides—must be perfectly symmetrical and of equal weight.

For a kite made out of notebook paper, a frame made of broom straw is generally sufficient. For larger kites, however, nothing is better than sticks of bamboo, either cut up into pieces or left whole. To divide a piece of bamboo into even sticks, slit through the natural knots one at a time, and then make intermediate slits to connect the first ones. The entire length of the bamboo will split evenly (see Fig. 9).

If one of the ends of the frame is heavier than the other (this can occur on an uncut length of bamboo), you must be careful to place the heavier part on the bottom of your kite. You can then balance the horizontal support by tying a counterweight to the lighter end (see Fig. 10).

For a larger competition kite, construct a

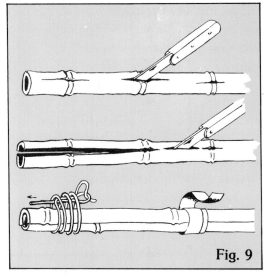

Fig. 9

well-balanced frame by slitting the bamboo as previously described, and then by reversing the two ends before rejoining them by whipping or taping them together (see Fig. 9). Place the exposed part of the slit bamboo on the side that supports the sail.

You can assemble the parts for a small kite's frame either by crossing them over and bending a pin around them or by surrounding the joint with adhesive tape.

For large kites, connections made of thread or string must be utilized. Use several drops of glue to hold the joints in place.

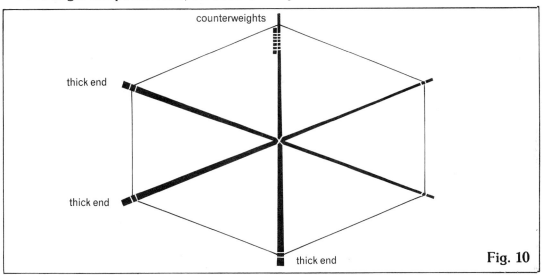

counterweights

thick end

thick end

thick end

Fig. 10

If the frames of your kite cross at right angles, use a square connection; otherwise, you can use an X-shaped connection.

Construct a square joint as follows (see Figs. 11 and 12):

• Make a knot as shown in Fig. 11 on one of the supports.

• Pass the string three times around, alternately over and under the supports.

• Twist the end once or twice to ensure the tightness.

• Make a final knot as shown (see top right of Fig. 11).

Make an X-shaped joint as follows (see Figs. 11 and 12):

• Make a horizontal knot as shown in Fig. 11.

• Wrap the string three times around vertically.

• Wrap the string three times around horizontally.

• Twist the cord around once.

• Make a final knot as shown.

Attach the rope at the outer edges of the supports by using knots that are placed in notches you cut in the ends of the supports (see Fig. 8).

Be sure the frame rests perfectly flat (except kites whose wings purposely raise).

The sail of a large kite can be controlled by complementary ropes (Fig. 8).

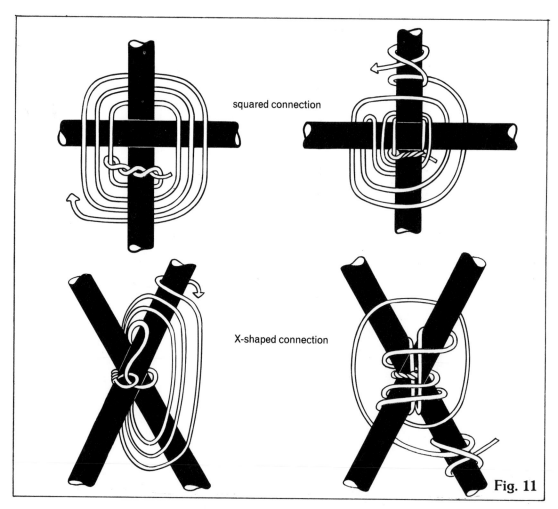

squared connection

X-shaped connection

Fig. 11

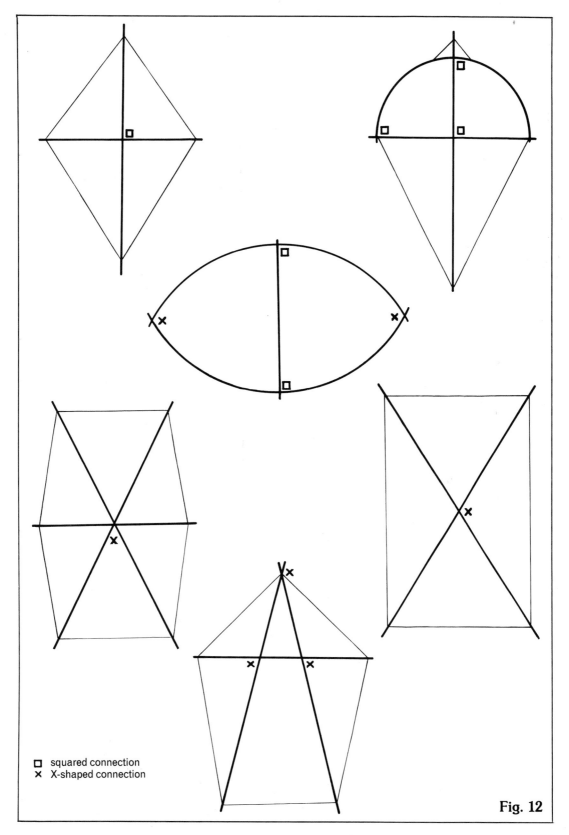

□ squared connection
✗ X-shaped connection

Fig. 12

Sail

The surface and type of kite you plan to make determine your choice of paper for the sail. Lay your chosen paper out flat. Place the frame on top of the paper and cut out the kite, leaving a sufficient margin to be glued and pulled over the rope or the outer support.

This margin must be as thin as possible so as to avoid unnecessary weight. To do this, smear the supports with a quick-drying glue, apply the paper on top and, after the glue is dry, cut off any excess paper that projects (see Fig. 13).

In the corners of big kites, as well as at the places where the frame crosses the sail, it might be necessary to glue small paper reinforcements, as shown in Fig. 13. This is because sometimes, when a kite is lifted up into the air by a great gust of wind, the sail could be torn off the frame. Several small paper or adhesive-tape tabs, just enough to keep the sail flat on the frame, are sufficient. It is unnecessary to cover the entire length of the supports in this way (see Fig. 13).

Tail

The role of the tail is to lower the center of gravity of the kite so that it can achieve a better altitude. The tail is the stabilizer that permits the kite to straighten itself up after it begins to fall due to a gust of wind. The weight of the tail is not nearly as important as its length. Depending on the strength of the wind, the length of the tail can be seven to ten (or even fifteen) times as long as the body of the kite itself. The stronger the wind, the longer the tail must be. It is therefore important to anticipate this while you are making the tail: Include several toggle pins and loops so that you can add additional length to the tail when needed. You could have, for example, a tail 6 yards (6 metres) long, ending in a large pompon, and several auxiliary pieces about 1, 2 or 3 yards (1, 2 or 3 metres) long that you can add and adjust as necessary.

If your kite has its spine underneath the sail, you can attach the tail directly to it; otherwise, you can consider adding a bridle to the kite's two lowest supports.

Some types of kites do not need to have tails at all; we discuss these types a little later.

The classic tail consists of paper curls. Its

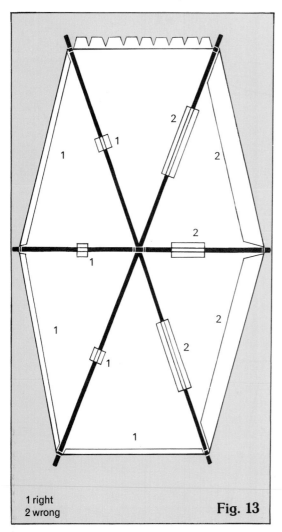

1 right
2 wrong

Fig. 13

main inconvenience is that the paper can easily get so tangled that it cannot be fixed. An alternative type of tail can be made out of continuous strips of paper that are placed end to end and glued around a piece of string. After the paper is glued in place, you can fringe it (see Fig. 14) to give it a better hold on the wind. Fig. 14 also shows how to attach this type of tail to the kite.

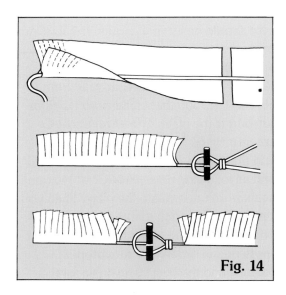

Fig. 14

Bridles

Depending on the type of kite, the bridles can either be double, triple or quadruple in number. Certain types of kites attach directly to the flying line and require no bridles at all.

The method of attaching the bridles to a kite is essential. An excellent kite, badly attached to the bridles, will never rise up, or it may begin to nose-dive or tail-spin. The way to decide where to attach the bridles involves complicated mathematics; base your measurements on the results of patient experimentation, observation and deduction.

One engineer has devised an empirical method for determining the point at which the line must pull. His method, described below, concerns kites without tails.

First you must find the center of tension—that is, the geometric middle of the sail. To do that, cut out a paper mock-up exactly to scale. Fold the paper along the back spine and then experiment to find the spot where the model balances perfectly on a pointed stem. This gives you point P, which you should transfer onto the kite itself (see Fig. 15).

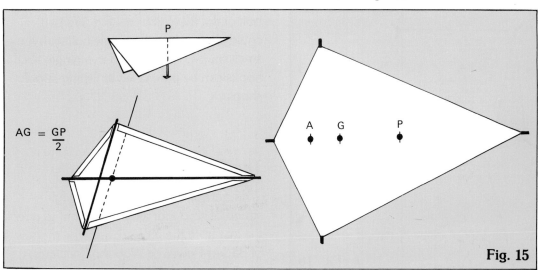

Fig. 15

To find the center of gravity G on the kite, stretch a piece of string horizontally. You are looking for the place at which the kite placed over the string attains perfect balance.

Point A is the place to which the prolonged flying line must extend. A is located along the elongation of line PG; line AG is one-half the length of GP.

In the case of a double fastening (two bridles), it is a good idea to make the length of each bridle at least equal to the distance that separates their connection points. Bridles are often too short; you must then lengthen them in order for the flight of the kite to proceed effectively.

Even with a perfect attachment, the action point of the flying line can be displaced at any moment by a gust of wind. In order to remedy that, place a piece of elastic onto the bottom bridle. This allows the cord to rapidly snap back to its original position after having yielded to the wind; see Fig. 16.

Because adjusting the length of the different bridles is quite a delicate procedure, you should equip yourself with a gadget to make this task easier, such as a plate to which you can separately attach the different bridles.

The rest of this section will describe how to make the adjustment plate for three bridles illustrated in Fig. 17. It is easy to adapt this gadget to fit kites with more or fewer bridles.

To begin, you need a small plate made of wood, bamboo or lightweight metal that is pierced with five lined-up holes. Each hole should be just big enough to allow the bridles to pass through it. The two upper reins A and B, which you make from the same string, enter the second hole from above. The loop that comes through then surrounds the plate. The lower bridle C enters into the first hole from underneath and then successively passes into the third and all following holes, finally coming out again from underneath the plate. Then you simply slide through this gadget whichever bridle is needed to either be lengthened or shortened in order to ensure proper balance and the best flying angle for the kite.

You should end the bridle with a loop or ring into which you can insert the toggle bolt of the flying line; see Fig. 17. You could also replace the toggle bolt with a small snap-hook attached to a hinge; such hooks can be purchased at fishing-supply shops.

The Flying Line

Generally, the flying line is a single strand of cord, but when you want to direct the kite from the ground, as in the models of Baden-Powell or Woodbridge Davis, it can be doubled. Maillot's kite even had

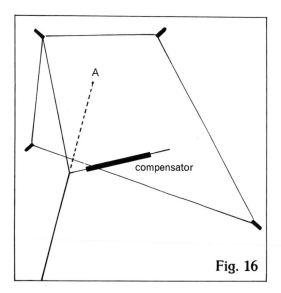

A

compensator

Fig. 16

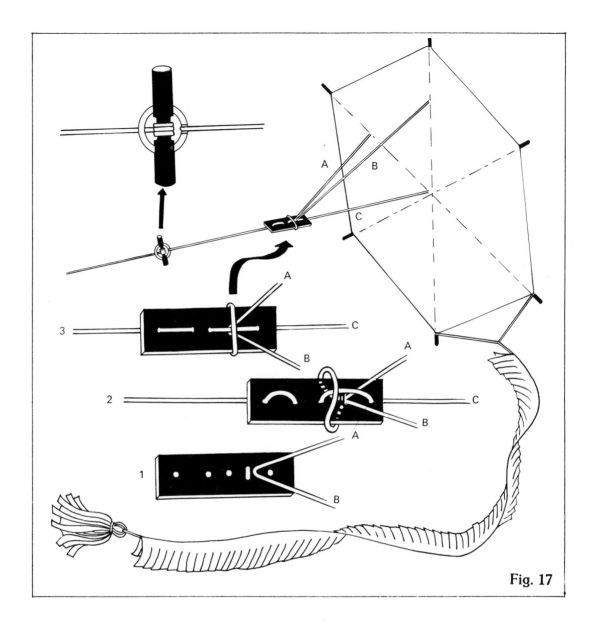

Fig. 17

seven flying lines. In such an instance, of course, manipulating the kite requires a certain amount of training so that you do not tangle up the entire arrangement.

Refer back to the section on equipment on page 14 to see what types of materials you can use to make the flying line.

You can lengthen the life span of a flying line considerably if you rub it in some melted wax. Once the wax is dry, polish the line with a piece of wool. This serves to hold the fibres of the cord together and to protect it from humidity. The worst thing that happens to a line is that it unravels, either from constantly passing through your hands or from rubbing against the stick that you have wound it around. Not only does this friction form ringlets in the cord which are impossible to fix, but it also untwists the cord itself, which results in a loss of strength. To avoid this, wind the cord around a reel with a crank.

Reel

There are many different types of reels around which you can wind the flying line, ranging from a very simple one composed of two off-centered handles to a model you place on the ground and control with a foot brake. One type, shown in Fig. 19, attaches around the waist. Use your imagination to create an appropriate reel for your kite; see Figs. 18, 19, 20, 21 and 22 for ideas.

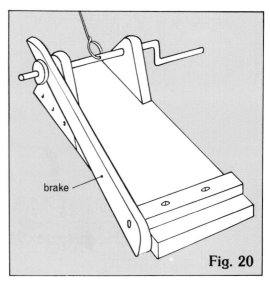

brake

Fig. 20

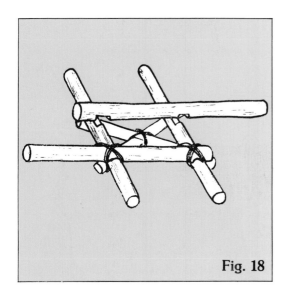

Fig. 18

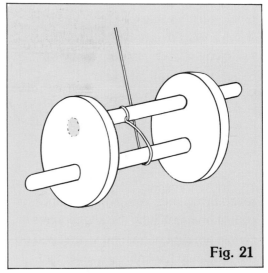

Fig. 21

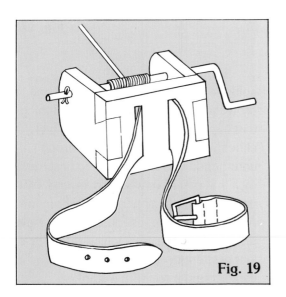

Fig. 19

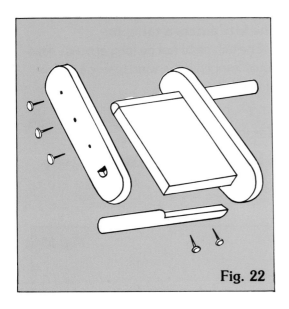

Fig. 22

possibly be better for achieving record altitudes. Sailing experts know quite a bit about air currents and the advice they can give you is invaluable to your kite-flying.

Recalling the Kite

To bring in your kite quickly (in the case of a storm or injury, for example), you need an aide to help hold the line, or you can attach the line to a fixed point. Pass your arms over the cord so that it strikes you under the armpit, and run in the direction of the kite. This pulls the kite right down (see Fig. 23 on page 26).

Launching the Kite

The most important condition necessary for the takeoff of your kite is sufficient wind near the ground; if there is not enough wind, you must be able to find an open area large enough to allow you to create a wind by running fast. It is fairly rare that over a height of about 30 yards (30 metres) there will not be sufficient wind to hold up a kite. The best method of launching a kite is to unroll about 50 yards (50 metres) of line and have a helper ready to release the kite into the wind at a given signal. The helper should simply let go of the kite, and not throw it into the air.

There are certain places that are impossible to use for the takeoff of kites: clearings in the woods, hollows in mountainsides, busy streets, river banks and other places where air holes and whirlwinds exist. In such places, you risk having the kite brutally and abruptly fall to the ground. On the other hand, certain edges of plateaus determine ascending air drafts and could not

Causes of Failure

Despite the wind, the kite does not go up, or it stays up unsteadily in the air:
The length or places of attachment of the bridles are miscalculated. Try lengthening or shortening the bridles.

The kite struggles in every direction, or it flips over on its back:
Nothing happens—that is, the kite is lying too flat in the wind. Shorten the bottom bridle to make the kite stand up and thus to give it a better hold on the wind. The kite will also be held back if the flying line is too heavy: In such a case, the kite goes up and the line curves.

The kite falls gently:
There is insufficient wind to keep the kite up. Try to run to raise up the kite, hoping to encounter sufficient air current.

The kite always overturns to the same side:

The kite is asymmetrical or one side (the side towards which it falls) is too heavy. To remedy this situation, attach a counter-weight to the opposite side. The bridle might also be too short (on the side towards which the kite falls).

The kite enters a tailspin:

The tail might not be long enough. This could happen if the wind tears off a piece of the tail (see Fig. 24).

Repairs

In the Far East, some people are very

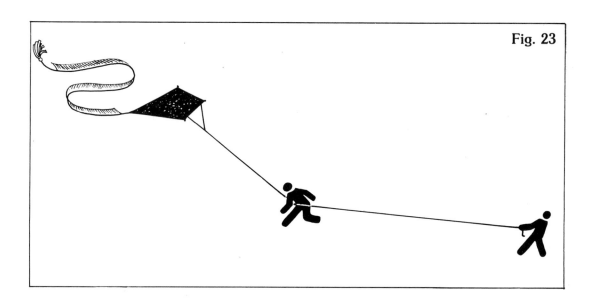

Fig. 23

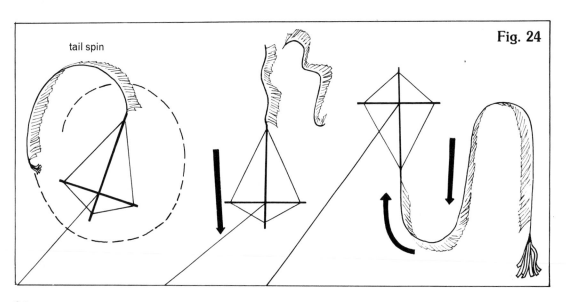

tail spin

Fig. 24

attached to the kites they have made. Whether this is because of their kites' performance or beauty, people try to save their creations. When an accident damages their kites, they try to repair them. In Sri Lanka, we saw kites flying that were composed of a multitude of abandoned pieces that fanatics searched for and reassembled.

We would like to encourage this practice. With a little bit of taste in carefully choosing the shape and colors of the pieces, you can form a beautiful patchwork design. You can also repair a broken frame with a splint attached with thread or adhesive tape. In this way, you can restore the kite's balance with an invisible repair from the back.

TYPES OF KITES

Simple Models

The various models described here are so simple that you can make them and have them flying in ten minutes. Even someone less skillful can, in only a little more time, create a finished product—without anyone else's help—and the kite will fly!

The Capuchin

This kite is very popular among Algerian children. We do not know whether the name of the kite comes from the fact that it resembles one of the bizarre grasshoppers that are found in North Africa, which are called "capuchins," or from its silhouette, which resembles that of a Capuchin monk.

There is no simpler construction than that required to create this kite. All you do, in effect, is to fold a small trumpet shape in one of the small corners of a piece of notebook paper. Hold the shape in place by means of a long twig or pin. This also serves as the place to attach the flying line of the kite. To complete the capuchin,

attach a tail that you can make from strips of paper pinned end to end (see Fig. 25).

The Glider

This kite originated in Morocco and can be made from a sheet of notebook paper cut into a square. After folding the square as shown in steps 1, 2, 3 and 4 in Fig. 26, spread out the square and attach a two-stranded bridle as shown.

As for the capuchin, make a tail consisting of strips of paper attached end to end.

The Wind Fairy

This kite hardly differs at all from the capuchin, except that it is even easier to make. It consists of a single long strip of paper that is folded into a trumpet shape in the middle. As in the capuchin, the trumpet is held in place by a pin. Use a second pin to attach the string that will be used to fly the kite; see Fig. 27 on page 32.

The Tadpole

This type of kite is closer to a "true kite" because it contains a frame.

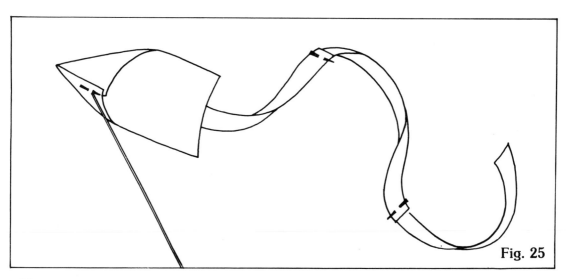

Fig. 25

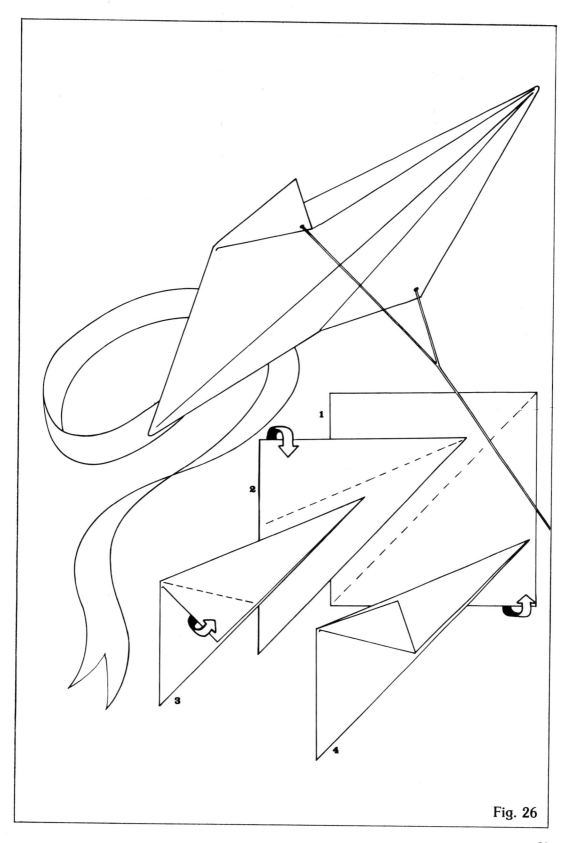

Fig. 26

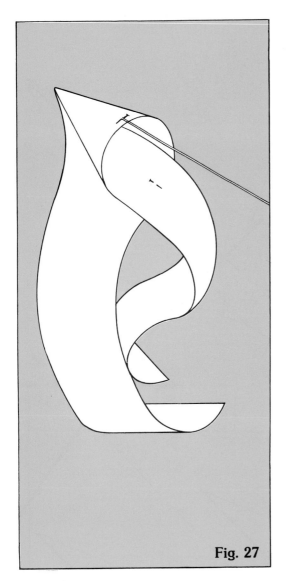

Fig. 27

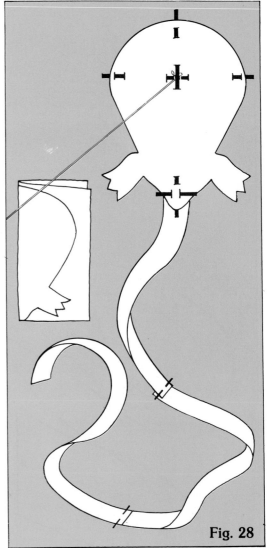

Fig. 28

Fold a piece of notebook paper in half so that you can cut out the two sides absolutely symmetrically. Use your imagination to create whatever shape tadpole you wish. Use a punch to make holes through which you thread the supports (see Fig. 28). Make the supports from strands of straw which can be pulled out from a broom; try to pick the straightest straws. You could also make the frame from reed sticks or pieces of bamboo that have been slit as thinly as possible.

Here are some helpful hints for the threading and placing of the supports on the paper:

1. The longest length of the frame must appear on what will be the upper side of the kite in order to support the paper as the wind strikes it.

2. A small crossbar must be formed under and in the middle of the kite so that you can attach the flying line there.

Put the sticks in place with adhesive tape.

The maximum size of this kite is about that of a single sheet of newspaper. If you use this larger size, you must make the supports from pieces of slit reeds.

After you finish the body, attach strips of paper end to end for the tail (Fig. 28 shows how to do this).

The tadpole, like all other lightweight kites, cannot fly in too strong a wind, since the supports could break.

Even in a light breeze, however, a tadpole can attain a respectable height; you can probably unroll about 475 yards (475 metres) of medium-weight string.

The Shooting Star

The principle for constructing this kite is the same as that for the tadpole, but only the shape is different. To ensure perfect symmetry, fold a piece of paper in quarters before cutting out the shape. You then need two cross supports made of straw. Use your imagination in cutting out a fanciful tail (Fig. 29).

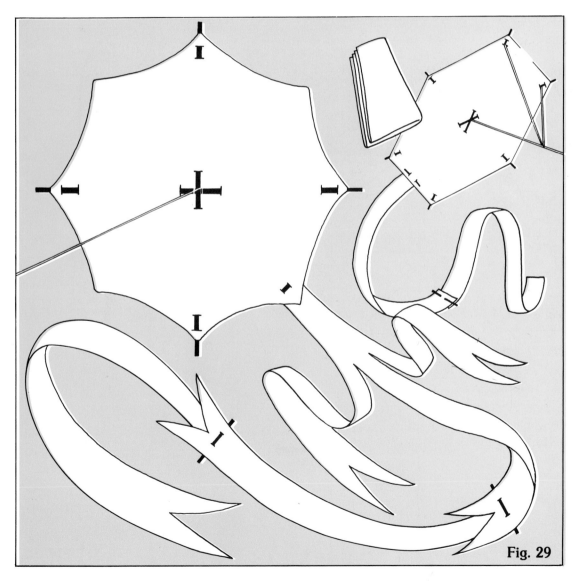

Fig. 29

After you have made a tadpole and a shooting-star kite, you can see that it is easy to invent other more or less complicated kite designs. (For example, see the hexagon shown in Fig. 29 on page 33.)

The Dutch Flyer

Here is another kite that can be made from a sheet of paper. The drawings in Fig. 30 indicate how to fold and cut the paper.

Begin by folding the longitudinal vein, which leads the little tongue a over a'. Fold the cross vein, pinning each end so that the fold does not open. Finally, glue on two "riders," each reinforced with a small twig as shown. Fasten the bridle of the kite to these twigs.

If your kite is perfectly balanced, you can do without a tail. If necessary, however, you can always add one.

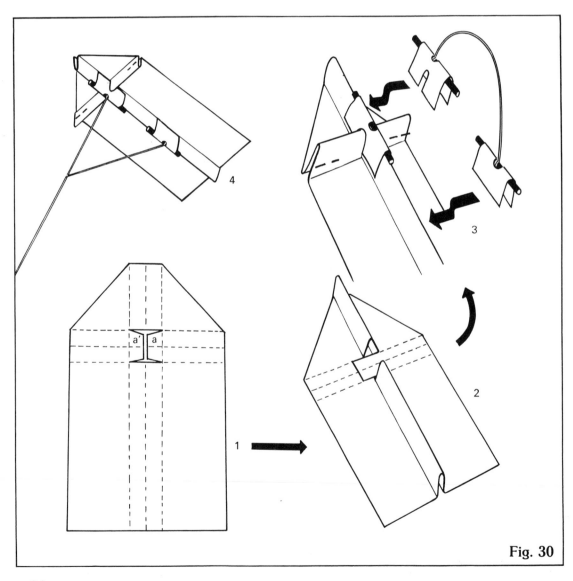

Fig. 30

The Flying Beast or Dragon

We now complicate things a bit by introducing a whimsical box kite.

It is recommended that this kite be made from lightweight kraft (brown) paper so that it can maintain a strong enough hold against the wind.

Cut out the general shape by following the drawing in Fig. 31. Notch the wings as shown. In this example, we have left the notches shaped very simply. Through each notch, thread a lightweight support to give each section the necessary rigidity. Fold over the edges of the paper to form the cells, and fasten the bottom with another support to which you then attach the bridles.

You can make a tail from cutout paper streamers resembling banners. Lengthen each wavy streamer by pinning the necessary strips end to end, and paint a design on the kite.

Kites with Glued Supports

To make this Indochinese kite, which should not exceed 24 inches (60 cm)

across, you need paper strong enough that neither rope nor supports are necessary for strength along the edges. Thin slits of bamboo glued directly to the back of the paper give sufficient support to the kite. The arrangement of these sticks can vary considerably—it depends on the cutout shape of the kite. Place one of the sticks along the central axis and then use two wire hinges to attach a movable wing to this central axis. This wing replaces the bridle on the underside of the kite. Reinforce the edges of this movable paper wing by glueing on two strands of rattan as shown in Fig. 32 on page 36.

To ensure perfect symmetry, fold the paper in half before cutting out your design. How many supports to use, and how to arrange them are not difficult problems to resolve at all!

Kites with Tails

The Pear

The pear is a well-known classic kite model which is not difficult to construct.

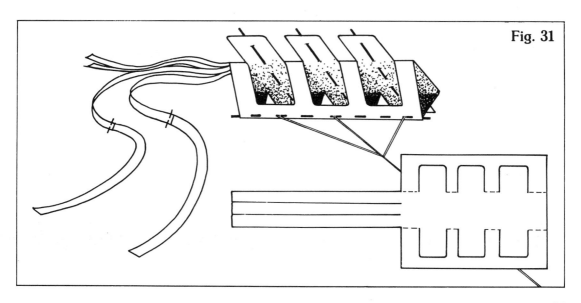

Fig. 31

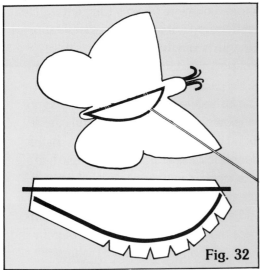

Fig. 32

Fasten the two-stranded bridle to the back spine, about one-fifth of the way down from the top of the kite and one-third of the way up from the bottom. Placed flat on the sail, the two strands should meet a little below the end of the curved support (*see* Fig. 33).

One young boy, inspired by the pear kite, invented a flexible kite made from the remains of an umbrella. His device could even fly in a strong wind! See Fig. 34.

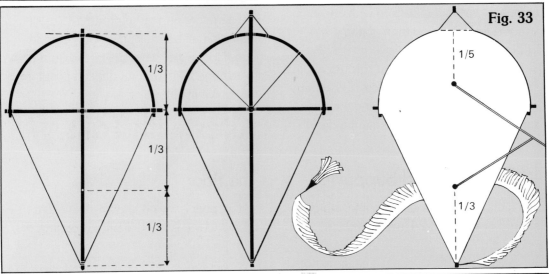

Fig. 33

1/3

1/3

1/3

1/5

1/3

The frame consists of a back spine. At a distance about one-third of the way from the top, a support frame is joined in a cross. Curve another flexible support over this first assembly. If necessary, ensure the evenness of the curve by adding complementary cords at the top (*see* Fig. 33).

This type of kite generally has a ''beak,'' though it is not an absolutely necessary part of the kite.

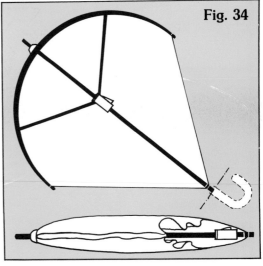

Fig. 34

The Hexagon

The hexagonal kite is one of the easiest of this type to make and to fly. Its frame· consists of two large supports and a shorter one, all of which cross at their middles.

To ensure the symmetry of your kite, the cording that forms the outer edge must start at one of the large supports and then must attach to the smallest. The length thus obtained is carried over to the next side. Keep the cord evenly stretched, as shown in Fig. 35.

For this type of kite, attach a three-stranded bridle to the topmost parts of the larger supports and to their crosspoint. If your kite is very big, attach the upper bridles slightly lower to reduce the strain on the supports.

If you modify the length of the supports and assemble them in different ways, you can create many other types of hexagons; however, the symmetry might be a little more difficult to obtain. You will also have to carefully consider exactly where to place the bridles, depending on the individual shape; see Fig. 36 and Fig. 36A.

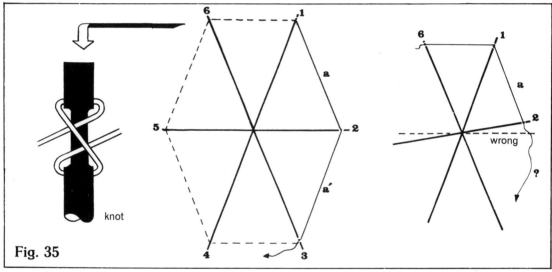

Fig. 35

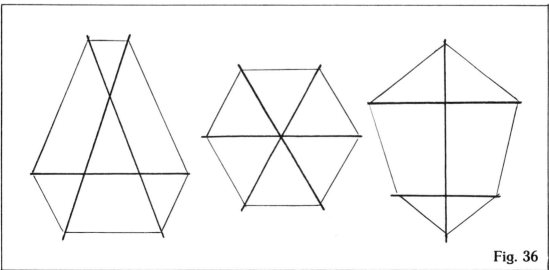

Fig. 36

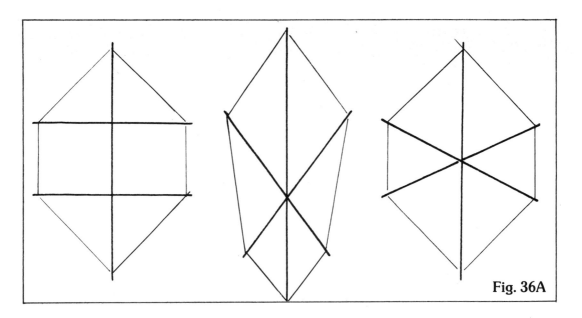

Fig. 36A

The Pentagon

To make a pentagonal kite like the one shown in Fig. 37, carefully measure the three supports needed for the frame. Assemble the three pieces as shown by using X-shaped joints.

The bridle should have four strands. Fasten two to the ends of the cross-support and the other two to the bottom of the remaining two supports.

The Russian Kite

This kite is a parallelogram that is slightly longer than it is wide—for example 1½ yards by 1¼ yards (1.5 metres by 1.25 metres).

The frame consists of a square made from four supports that are reinforced by two others that cross the square diagonally. To reduce the weight of the frame, you can make the two side supports from cord.

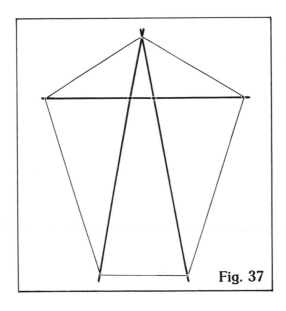

Fig. 37

After you put on the sail, connect the upper ends of the top support by a spreader AB, which curves the sail. The sag of the arch thus formed should be about ten percent of the width of the kite.

Russian children often add a strip of folded paper that snaps in the wind to the spreader (see Fig. 38). The origin of this practice can probably be traced to the Far East.

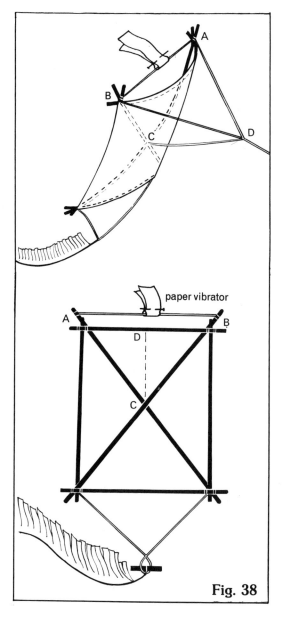

paper vibrator

Fig. 38

The Flying Disc

To make the flying disc shown in Fig. 39, see the instructions for the Chinese dragon kite on page 56. The flying disc is the head of the dragon with a tail attached.

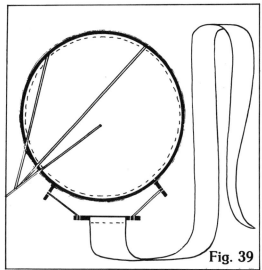

Fig. 39

The Flying Ghost

This fantastic kite was invented in a British colony in order to liven up a grand tournament that took place around the ruins of an old castle.

To help you understand the construction of this magnificent creation, Fig. 40 illustrates the sail on one side and the plain frame on the other. Three long strips of netting, fastened at the feet and at the ends of the wings, give the illusion of trains, while serving as tails.

At night, lit up with the help of a flashlight hidden by the flying line, the flying ghost creates a powerful impression.

Kites without Tails

There are three categories of kites without tails: kites whose wings are raised up by a spreader; kites with pockets through which the air passes; and streamlined kites.

Fig. 40

Most of the frames of these models have a bamboo back spine and are completed with supports made from rattan. Soak the rattan for a few minutes; this allows you to then form it easily into any shape you wish. Let the shape dry on a wooden plank; stick pins into the rattan in various places to ensure that it maintains the desired shape.

The sails of some kites are made of rice paper. A coat of varnish reinforces the paper after it is shaped. Because this paper is fragile when it is wet, be careful not to put glue on the part you will fold over, but put it instead on the part that will receive the other piece. Your work will thus be much easier because the covering remains dry and is easier to manipulate. The simplest way to do this is to smear glue on the support and to place the paper flat on top of it. Cut off any excess paper after the glue dries (see Fig. 41).

Kites with a Wing Spreader

The wings of these kites are raised up by a spreader. When the kite flies from side to side, the air is prevented from overturning the kite.

The Japanese Kite

To begin this kite, you need a back spine. To the ends of this spine, you must connect from their midpoints two additional supports which join up at their ends (Fig. 42). The spreader creates a type of

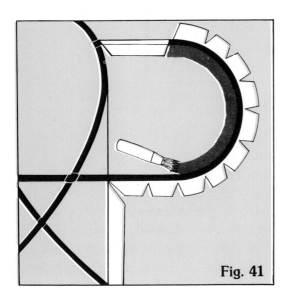

Fig. 41

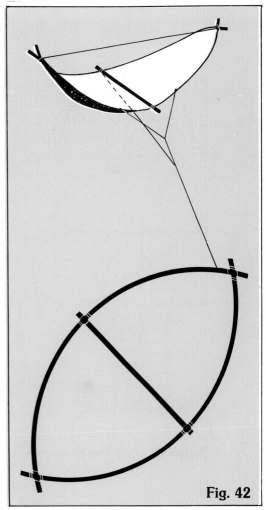

Fig. 42

flying wing. As you can see in the drawing, the bridle for this kite is somewhat unusual. The two strands that end the upper bridle allow you to regulate the balance of the kite and to compensate, if necessary, for the tendency the kite has to nose-dive to one side. To adjust for this, you can lengthen or shorten the point of attachment on the wing concerned.

The Thai fighting *papkao* (page 11) is constructed in the same fashion as this kite, but a very long cloth tail is added that is about five times the length of the back spine.

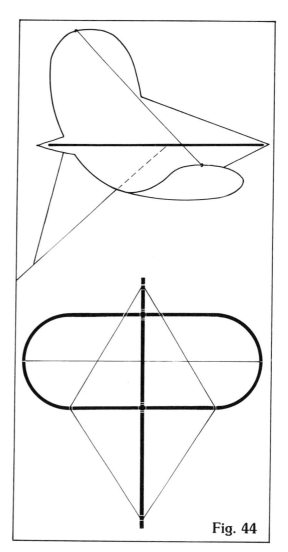

Fig. 44

The Vietnamese Kite

In Indochina, the Vietnamese kite can take a variety of shapes; Figs. 43 and 44 show two examples. Generally, the frame consists of a single stiff bamboo support that forms the back spine. All the other supports are made from rattan and are kept in place with a network of lightweight thread. A sail can be made from rice paper, ensuring that the kite is extremely light and that it can go up even with the slightest puff of air.

Add a spreader to raise up the wings (see Figs. 43 and 44).

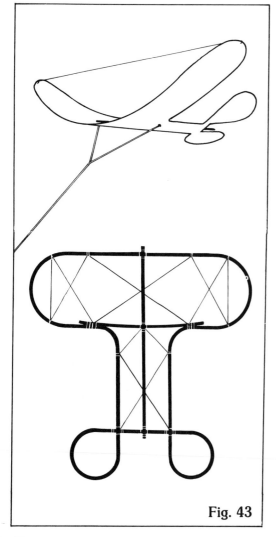

Fig. 43

Despite its simple appearance, this is not a kite for beginners to attempt. The biggest problem it presents is how and where to fasten the bridles. Sometimes this requires long and discouraging experimentation. Only after trying out different types of bridles—of various lengths and points of connection—can you succeed in placing them. It is certainly worth the trouble, however, to fly this lightweight kite.

The Japanese Bird

The kite whose frame is illustrated in Fig. 45 is constructed according to the same principles as the Vietnamese kite. Place the spreader on the cross-support that holds the wings.

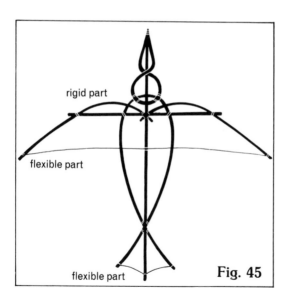

rigid part

flexible part

flexible part

Fig. 45

The Quadrilateral

Following are the relative proportions for the quadrilateral kite shown in Fig. 46 based on the longest piece AB. Other pieces are shown in tenths of AB. Thus, if

you make AB 10 inches (25 cm) long, XB should be 8 inches (20 cm) long.

$$AB = 10 \quad \begin{cases} AX = 2 \\ XY = 5 \\ YB = 3 \end{cases} \quad CD = 7 \quad \begin{cases} CX = 3.5 \\ XD = 3.5 \end{cases}$$

$$XB = 8$$

$$BC' = 8$$

$$AC' = AD'$$

$$BD' = 8$$

Connect the two supports crosswise where shown in Fig. 46, and then stretch

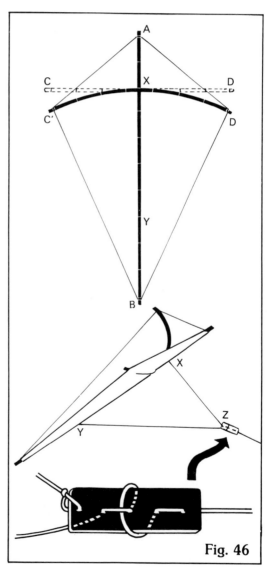

Fig. 46

CD into the arc of a circle using cords BC′ and BD′. Attach the continuation of both cords to A.

Because of the curved shape of the frame, you must cut the sail for this kite in two parts in order to place the front and the back part separately. First attach BC′XD′, being sure to cut side C′XD′ into an arc. Complete the kite with sail AC′XD′, which you can adjust as necessary.

The proportionate dimension of the bridle is XZ = 4.

YZ varies depending on the strength of the wind. To account for this, add a small regulating block, as shown in Fig. 46.

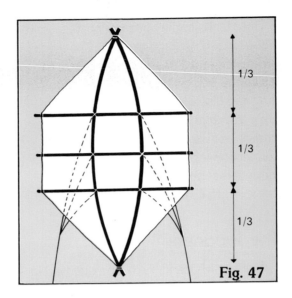

Fig. 47

Baden-Powell's Kite

Baden-Powell's first kite measured 11 yards (11 metres) in height and 6⅓ yards (6.35 metres) in width, and the frame was made from solid bamboo. You probably will not want to grapple with the arrangements necessary for such a large device! Instead, you could begin with a model ten times smaller—that is, about 1 yard (1 metre) by 2 feet (.65 metre).

Tie together two supports at the ends to form the back spine. The supports should be separated from each other in the middle, as shown in Fig. 47. Tie on two sticks crosswise, each about one-third of the way in from the end of the spine. Fasten a third stick between these two, as shown. Curve all three by support ropes.

Make the sail from cloth. When you sew it, be careful to leave enough slack so that the bottom triangle of the kite can rise powerfully in flight.

Baden-Powell's revolving kite was controlled by two flying lines attached to triple bridles. However, there is no reason why you cannot consider using one line.

Simple or Multiple Flying Arc

The frame of a simple flying arc consists of a back spine on which rest two crossed, tied-together supports (Fig. 48 shows the placement of the supports). Bend all three supports by means of a spreader.

Wrap a cord around the perimeter as shown. Add a square sail, which can be made out of either paper or cloth. The particular kite shown is attached to a bridle with three strands.

Using these same principles, you can construct a flying arc with several sails on a single spine; the drawing on the right in Fig. 48 illustrates one example.

"Chula"

The "chula" is the combat kite of Thailand (see page 11) and so its decoration is usually limited to the insignia of the particular club it represents.

The kite itself, which includes a spreader for the wings, can measure 2 or 3 yards (2 or 3 metres), and sometimes more. Flying it, therefore, necessitates an entire drill

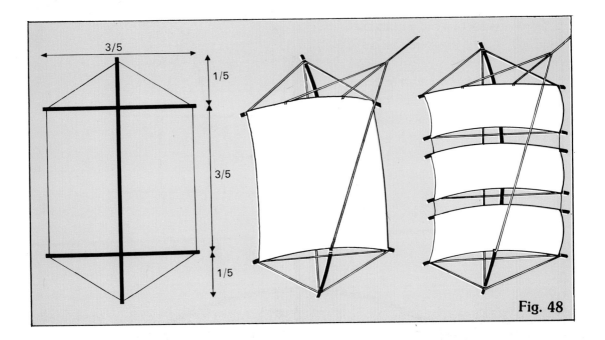

Fig. 48

team that a captain commands with a whistle. Even through you won't want to make such a large kite, you can make one to your requirements easily by referring to the diagram in Fig. 49 on page 46.

Kites with Pockets

Kites with pockets have no tails. Their stability is ensured by pieces that form a kind of parachute. This type of kite is trickier to make than the types previously discussed.

Japanese Fly

This creation is an example of a kite with pockets. The wings form the pockets.

The kite consists of a rigid surface made from a bamboo spine on which you tie a rattan "eight." Hold the eight in place with two lateral cords (Fig. 50, p. 47). Shape the rattan frame for the wings into an eight.

Complete the end of each wing with a circle slightly inclined towards the outside.

Make the sails for the rigid eight and the sail for the wings from lightweight paper—either tissue, rice or crepe. Note that if the paper you use for the body is stiff enough to keep the pocket in shape, the end circles are not necessary.

Chinese Pocket Kite

The principle behind this kite is exactly the same as for the Japanese fly. The only difference is that the stiff spine is perforated in the middle.

Fly with the Elevated Nose

You can make another type of Japanese fly, but this type has a body which curves in the shape of a boat hull instead of resting flat. Because this kite is somewhat tricky to construct, refer to Fig. 52 on page 49. As you will see later, this plan lends itself to many different interpretations.

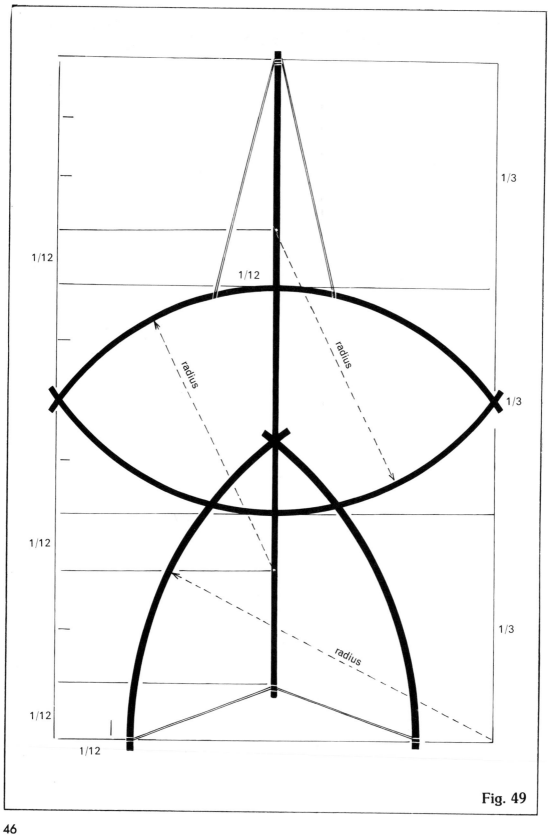

Fig. 49

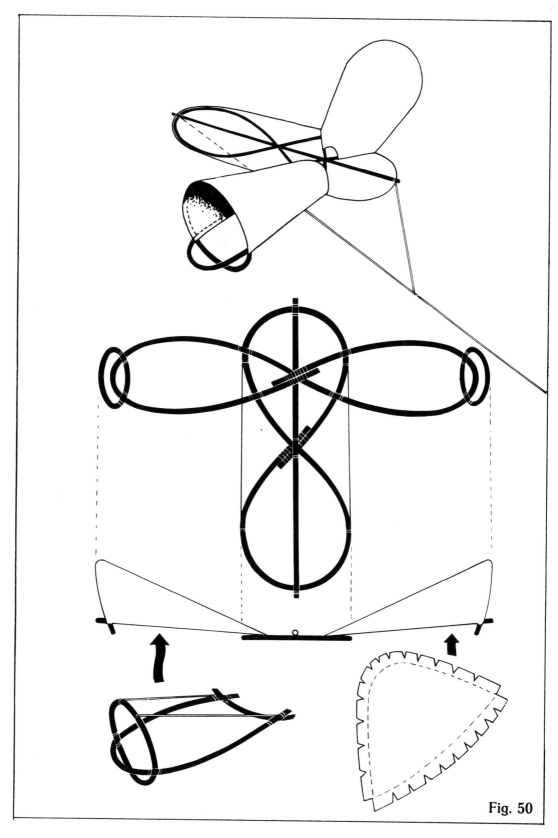

Fig. 50

You can make practically this entire project, assembly included, by enlarging the drawing in Fig. 52 to your chosen scale. For example, allow about 2 inches (5 cm) for every square in the diagram. Using thumbtacks, attach the diagram either to a drawing board or onto a table into which you can stick pins or make small holes.

Make the back spine ADB from a piece of split bamboo. Soak the bamboo in hot water and bend it to shape it to the angle you want. Place it into the pattern between two rows of pins so that it maintains the proper shape while drying.

Make the various supports from rattan. Soak them in water for five to ten minutes to soften them and then fasten them to the pattern, letting them dry as you did for the spine. After they are shaped and dried, tie the parts of the kite together with wire. Secure the joints with drops of glue (see Fig. 51).

Because of the contour of the hull, you must cut out each one of its sides separately (parts ABba). Glue the paper for the body under the spine from B to D, then under the supports from B to b to a.

With the aid of appropriate openings, shape the paper to best fit the curve of the nose and glue it on to AD and Aa. If the openings join poorly, cover them over with a thin strip of paper.

Make the covering of the wings (the grey part in the diagram) as follows:

1. Using a compass, start at C with a radius of C_1, equal to the height that the end of the pocket should be, and mark a spot to locate the position of C_1 and C_2.

2. From a, with a radius equal to the continuation of the straight line of the support ac, use a compass to cross-check the exact position of C_1.

3. Do the same thing from b to cross-check the location of C_2.

4. Point X is at the intersection of the continuation of C_1a and C_2b. From this point, use a compass to draw the outside edge C_1C_2 of the pocket.

5. Cut out the pocket sail. Glue it beginning from ab, then continuing on the inside of the supports for the wings. Connect the bridle at C and at B.

Fig. 53 shows you several modifications of the pattern given in Fig. 52 so that you can invent flies of very different character. All you need to do is to reverse the "hull," lengthen the spine or add in several supplementary supports. From there, you can use your imagination to create very personal variations.

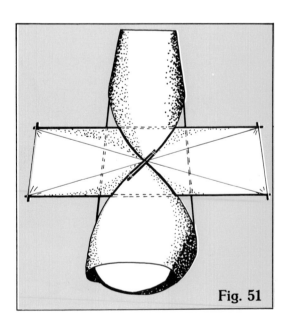

Fig. 51

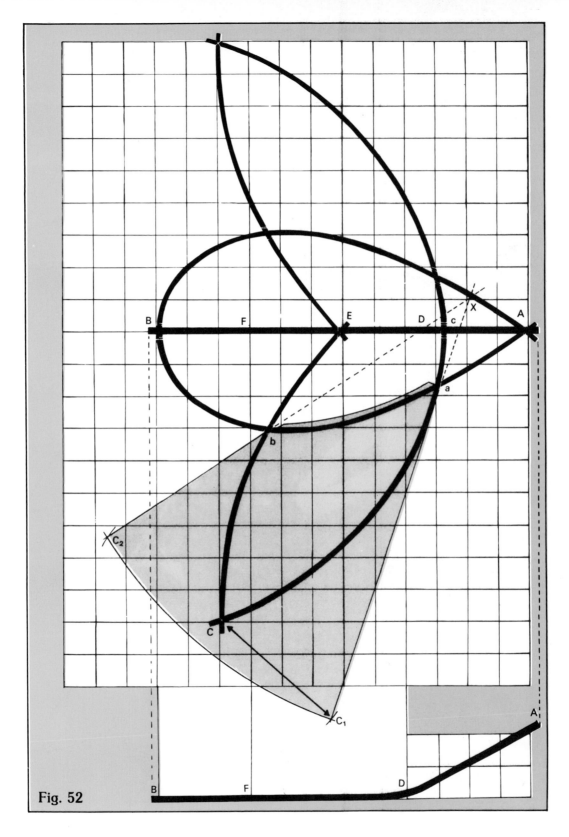

Fig. 52

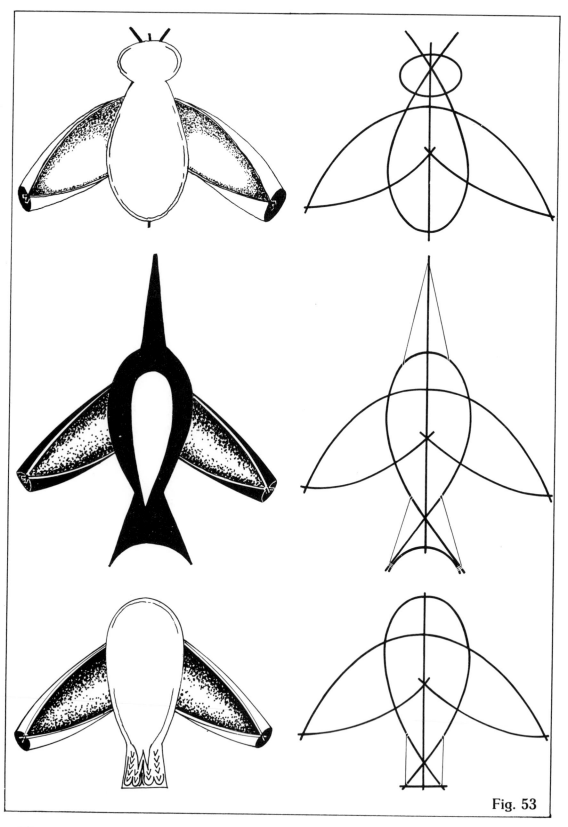

Fig. 53

Biot's Pocket Kite

Biot was probably inspired by the fly type of kite when he had the idea in 1880 to invent a kite equipped with two side funnel-like projections. He attached a freely turning propellor to his kite—a propellor whose rotation compensated for the absence of a tail (see Fig. 54).

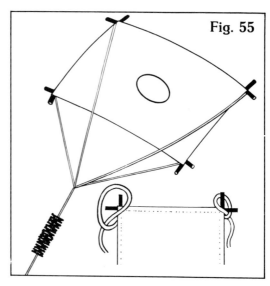

Fig. 55

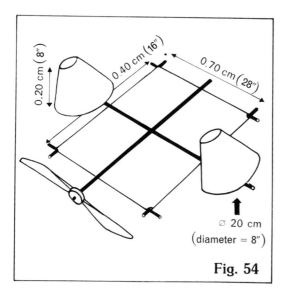

Fig. 54

The Korean Kite

Strictly speaking, this is not a kite with pockets, but it resembles one in that it has a hole in its sail through which the air passes (see Fig. 55). The directions presented below are based on the original Korean kite.

The Koreans use this kite to organize competitions. Certain parts of the flying line are passed through a mixture of glue and coarse-grained sand. Using skillful manoeuvres, the competitors strive to put their opponents out of combat by cutting their lines.

The frame of this kite is rectangular and is formed from four supports solidly tied at the four corners.

In the middle of the sail, which must be made from cloth and must curve towards the wind, cut out a relatively large circular hole through which air can escape. This hole is indispensable, because the kite will tip without it.

The following are some approximate proportions for this kite, however, you can make the kites any size.

length: about 15 inches (.40 metre)
width: about 13 inches (.35 metre)
hole: about 6 inches (.15 metre)

Attach a four-stranded bridle that is composed of two shorter and two longer cords to give an incline to the kite. To determine the exact placement and length of the bridles, you have to experiment and lengthen or shorten the two equal strands as necessary to balance the kite. You can easily shorten the strands by simply making some loops, as shown in Fig. 55, by passing the cord over the ends of the supports.

Jobert's Mooring-Line Carrier

This kite is composed of a square panel on the top of which you attach an open cone. The small opening should measure one-tenth of the diameter of the larger opening. Pass a spindle through the small hole. Fasten some thin strips of lightweight metal to the spindle; these strips wave freely, and the air that escapes through the small hole makes them vibrate, thus attracting the attention of survivors to be rescued.

Attach a bridle equipped with a ring; see Fig. 56. This allows you to transport a lifesaving rope which serve either to tow a buoy or to haul a heavier line.

Original Creations

The most interesting moment is the one at which you begin to transform existing designs into your own. Jobert's line carrier lends itself well to such adaptations. By adding certain pieces that the wind can move about and thus highlight, you can create many fascinating variations of the kite shown in Fig. 56.

Another amusing variation you can try is to make the hexagon kite described on page 37., remove its tail, and endow it with pockets, as shown in Fig. 57.

The more you experiment with different types, the more easily new ideas come to you. Have fun!

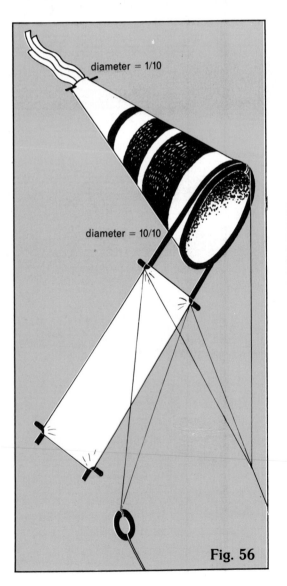

diameter = 1/10

diameter = 10/10

Fig. 56

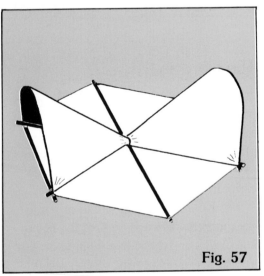

Fig. 57

Streamlined Kites

Streamlined kites are made, above all, to please the eyes. They are characterized by rattan frames that are entirely covered with paper and by wings that lift up in very open V-shapes.

The attachment of the wings to the frame differs depending on whether the two wings are interdependent on one another or whether they are made separately (see Fig. 58 on page 54).

Here is the method of construction to follow:

1. Draw a pattern to the full size you plan to make your kite. Attach your drawing to a drawing board or a panel of plywood.

2. Roll out a strip of dampened rattan along the outlines of your drawing. Keep it in place between some pins or small nails.

3. After the rattan is dry, tie and glue the points at which the rattan crosses.

4. Remove this armature from the plywood or drawing board so you can complete the hull, and assemble the various parts that you made separately.

5. Make a paper covering for the hull and the sail. Finish the kite by painting an artistic decoration using poster paints (see Fig. 59 on page 54).

Jointed Kites

This is an amusing type of kite composed of several movable parts that are assembled together. Once in the air, these kites take life by twisting and by flapping their wings or tail. Fig. 60 on page 55 shows several examples.

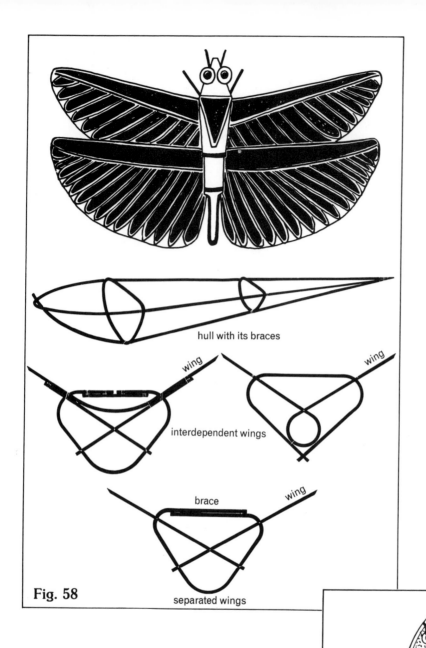

hull with its braces

wing
wing

interdependent wings

brace
wing

separated wings

Fig. 58

Fig. 59

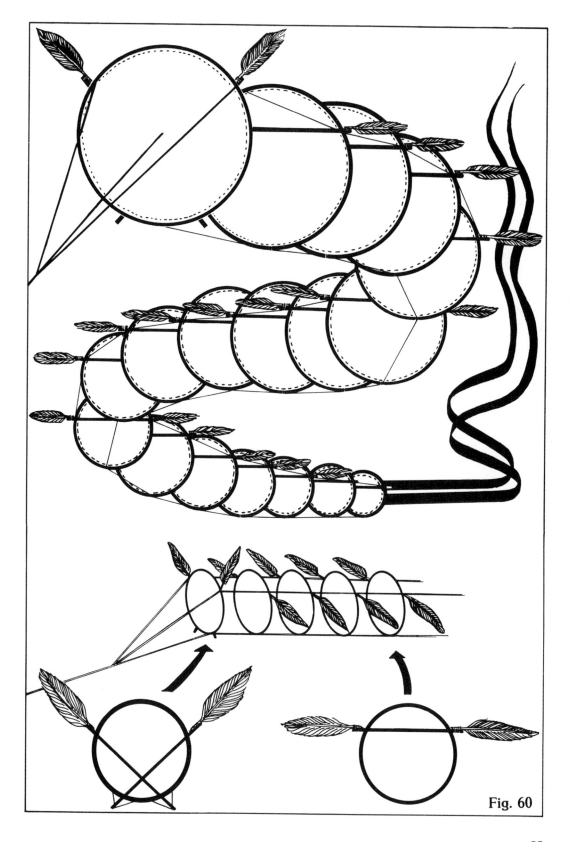

Fig. 60

The Chinese Dragon

The frame of this kite consists of a series of rattan circles covered with paper. Mount the circle for the head on a cross made of bamboo or cane. The additional circles diminish in diameter towards the tail. Tie these circles to a crossbar about one-third of the distance down from the top. Tie large feathers to the ends of the crossbars; these serve as balancing poles for the discs. To ensure the equilibrium of the dragon, you must place the joints of the rattan circles towards the bottom. Note that if the crossbars are too short or if they are placed too low, the dragon might not balance correctly.

Use three pieces of string to interconnect the discs to each other. Attach two at the top of the discs and one at the bottom, as shown in Fig. 60.

Fasten two long tails to the back of the dragon, and connect them to the crossbar on the last disc.

Make the triple-stranded bridle from the continuation of the three strings that connected the discs to each other.

The Chinese dragon can be very long, and it is therefore fairly difficult to launch. Once it is in the air, however, it is great fun to watch as it waves in the wind. If you paint it, you can give it a fantastic appearance.

The Raven from Sri Lanka

This kite was originally made in Ceylon, which is now known as Sri Lanka. When you make it from black paper and see it swirling in the air, you might even believe that you are seeing one of the ravens who swarm on that Far Eastern island.

If you proceed carefully and in a logical order, this kite is easy to make.

1. Begin by drawing a pattern in the full size you plan to make your kite. The pattern shown in Fig. 61 represents the frame on one side and the sail on the other.

2. Make the frames for the body and for the tail, including the legs. Make the supports from bent bamboo, whose measurements you take from the pattern you have made. Tie the end of the beak in an X, and all the other joints in a square.

3. Attach the sail for the body and that for the tail. To finish, glue short fringes to the end of the tail. You could also add a fringed border around the curved part of the body, as the Sri Lankans do. For decoration, you can also roll a strip of colored paper around each leg.

4. Attach the tail to the body with flexible joints at B and C. These joints must allow the two parts to move freely.

5. Make and attach the wings. Use a square of paper measuring the length of the spreader AB. You can reinforce the edges of the wings by folding them down and glueing them onto a strip of tape or piece of wire.

From a square of the same size as the wing, cut out the long fringe shown in Fig. 61. Glue this fringe so that it forms a continuation of the wing as shown. If you want to enhance the resistance of your kite to the wind, you can cut out and glue on two thicknesses of fringe. Use some adhesive tape between the two thicknesses to hold them together.

The fringe with which you edge the borders of the wings should not be as wide as the bottom fringe so that it does not get tangled with the fringe along the sides of the tail.

The Sri Lankans do not reinforce the wings and the fringe; they find it much

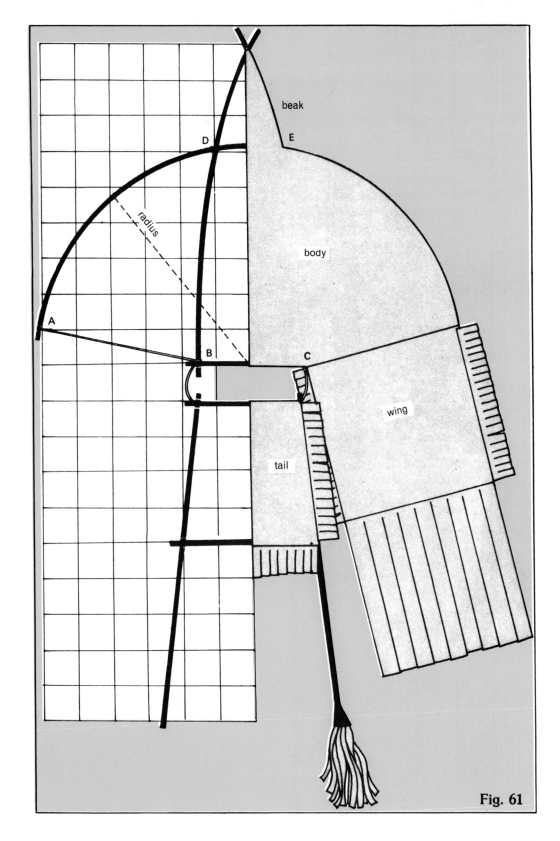

beak

D

E

radius

A

B

C

body

tail

wing

Fig. 61

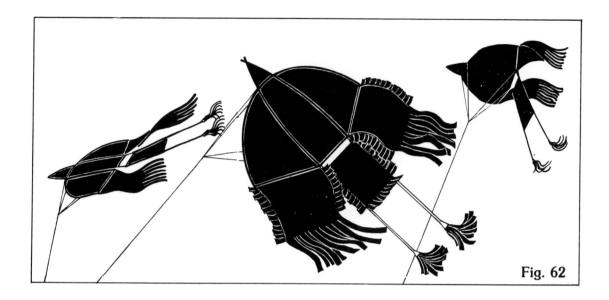

Fig. 62

easier to glue a patch over any torn area or to replace those parts ruined by the wind.

6. Attach the four-stranded bridle at B, C, D and E.

After you have completed your "raven" and it has demonstrated its aerial prowess, you are ready to create other types of birds, fish or other beings. Try making several quick drawings, which help you to visualize which parts of the raven you can easily change: You can, for example, lengthen the beak or legs, change the shape of the head by adding a circle of rattan, or add cords to modify the sail.

Do not be discouraged if your creative attempts do not meet with instantaneous success. When, after many tries, you finally create a model with which you are pleased, you will be very satisfied. Remember that you can then use your successful pattern as a point of departure for many additional discoveries. Your pattern can be used as follows:

...with the addition of floating wings;

...without floating wings, but with a wing spreader;

...with a simple beak or with a shape changed by cord AB;

...with a tail modified with cords or strips of rattan;

...with a tail completed by a floating portion;

...with a simple fringe or with rows of superimposed feathers.

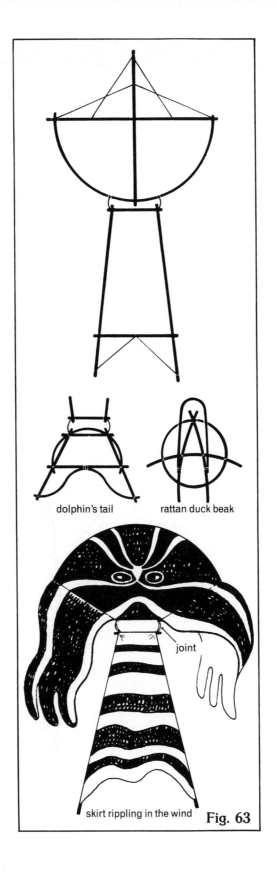

dolphin's tail

rattan duck beak

joint

skirt rippling in the wind

Fig. 63

59

USING THE KITE

The Dispatch

(Also called **Navigator** or **Pilot**)

When your kite is finally in the air, you can make and send up a "dispatch."

To make a simple dispatch, you need a circle of strong paper about 5 to 6 inches (12 to 15 cm) in diameter. Slit the circle along one of its radii, cutting out a small circular opening in the middle (see Fig. 64).

Once the kite is in the air, place this circle around the flying line. Pin it in the shape of a wide-open cone with the point towards the ground. The wind will whisk the cone up and away to the kite unless a knot or hitch in the cord stops it en route.

You can perfect your dispatch by adding a long, colored-paper streamer to the end. If you do this, it is not necessary to shape a cone at all because the wind—having taken hold of the paper streamer—prevents the dispatch from jumping off the line. This is an excellent way to send messages using differently colored "flames."

The Unfurling Cone

The problem with the type of dispatch described above is that it cannot slide back down the line. However, it is possible to unfurl the dispatch by using a special device that is not hard to make.

Take a piece of strong paper and roll it into a fairly tapered cone. Use a punch to pierce three holes in it, as shown in Fig. 65. Unroll the cone so that you can easily thread the flying line of the kite through the holes. That done, re-form the cone and stretch out the line. Note that the point of the cone must aim towards the dispatch (see Fig. 65).

Be sure to use a dispatch that is not closed (and that includes a streamer), whose central hole is large enough to allow the point of the unfurling cone to enter it easily. In pushing back on the streamer, the wind increasingly drives the dispatch into the cone. This helps pry open the slit and activates the unfurling.

If you write a message on the dispatch, you can see which part to retrieve after the unfurling.

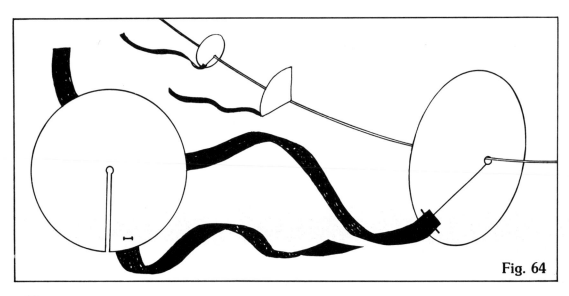

Fig. 64

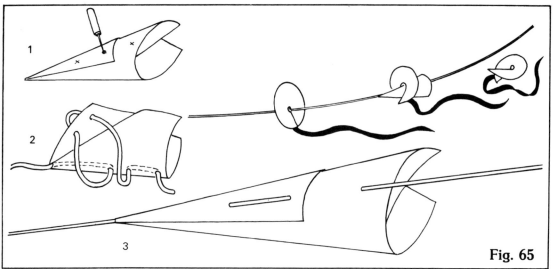

Fig. 65

Pilot with a Sail

Making a pilot with sails gives you the opportunity to use your imagination to invent numerous and varied models.

Essentially, a pilot consists of a pole which has a sail and two open rings that allow you to place the pilot on the flying line of a kite. Once the pilot is in place, the wind raises it up the line until it stops against an abutment placed especially for this purpose. As always, begin with an easy example.

A Simple Pilot

Follow Fig. 66 to make a very simple pilot. Make the pole, armature for the sail and the suspension rings from a single piece of metal wire; glue a paper sail onto the armature. To transmit a message, paint pilots different colors to correspond to coded flags. You can transmit your messages a long distance to a series of kite-flying friends who are equipped with binoculars. For even more fun, you can also invent a secret code!

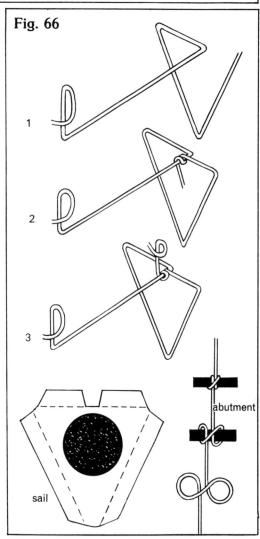

Fig. 66

sail

abutment

Pilot with a Floating Sail

This easy-to-make pilot consists of a triangular sail made rigid by a lightweight armature held in its edges. The upper support is held in the middle by a ring attached to the end of the pole. You can make the ring from strong thread or thin metal wire. Two fixed side cords prevent the sail from turning. A third cord, attached to the bottom of the triangle, ends in a loop that you pass onto the thrust rod to hold the sail (see Fig. 67).

rod on the sail lodges in a notch that has been carved at the end of the pole. Two side ropes hold the sail in this position. These ropes must be stretched sufficiently that they bend slightly in the manner of a bow. Attach a third rope, which forms a hanger, to the bottom of the sail and to a loop made especially for this purpose. When you unfurl the side ropes, the sail's support rod eases and projects the sail out of the notch. The sail hangs at the end of its hanger (see Fig. 68).

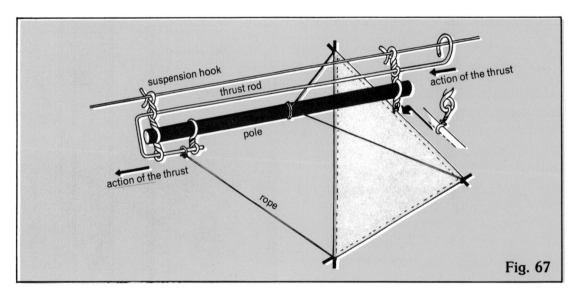

Fig. 67

When the pilot arrives at the end of the run, the rod is driven back. Because the bottom cord then becomes unfurled, the sail floats free and the pilot redescends.

However, if the wind is very strong, the sail will be too taut to allow the descent. You can weight the pilot just enough so that the sail has the strength to rise up very slowly.

Pilot with an Ejector Sail

In this model, the middle of the support

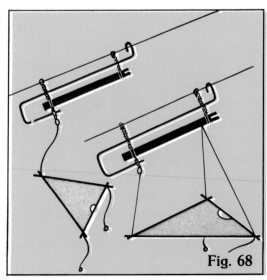

Fig. 68

An improvement on this design consists of adding two more hangers whose lengths are calculated so that the sail, once it is catapulted, hangs horizontally under the pilot, preventing the wind from taking hold (see Fig. 69).

Pilot with a Pivoting Sail

This model is composed of a sail that pivots when it is unfurled and that moves along the pole to resist the wind, thus facilitating the descent of the pilot.

Mount the sail on a wire frame that can pivot on a screw attached under and to the end of the rod. The sail has ropes attached to one of its sides and to its bottom. Both are connected to the same loop. When one of the ropes is unfurled, an elastic makes the sail pivot (see Fig. 70).

Fig. 70 shows a new way to attach the launching rod. This passes inside the pole, which is made of a tube of bamboo or strong cardboard. It is very easy to make a cardboard tube. Use a stick as a mould. Roll one or more pieces of newspaper that have been smeared with glue tightly around the stick. To be sure that the paper

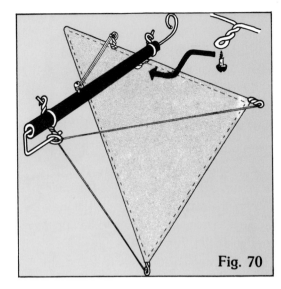

Fig. 70

does not adhere to the stick, first cover it with a piece of nonglued newspaper. After the glue is dry, remove the mould.

Pilot with a Vanishing Sail

The sail is equipped with a single rope at the end of which hangs a small sack of weights (see Fig. 71). When you loosen the loop of rope, the sack falls and lifts the sail up along the pole against which it holds the sail to lift it with the action of the wind.

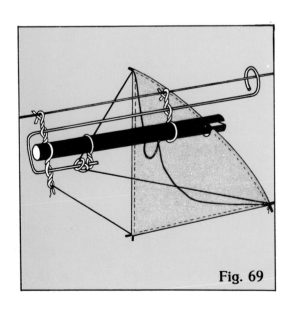

Fig. 69

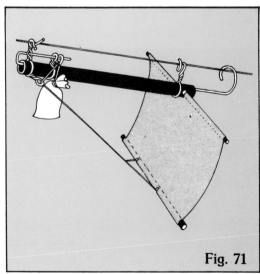

Fig. 71

The only precaution to take (besides the actual construction of this pilot) is to be sure that the pole is long enough that the sail can make way without being thwarted by the position of the sack of weights.

Pilot with a Short Pole

Instead of using a very long pole which is necessary to give sufficient recoil to the recall rope, attach a support to the midpoint of the sail. From there, fasten the rope at the height you judge to be appropriate (see Fig. 72).

For the model shown in Fig. 72, make sure that rope AB is shorter than CD so as to ensure that the sail vanishes completely. The length of the rope depends on the placement of points A and D.

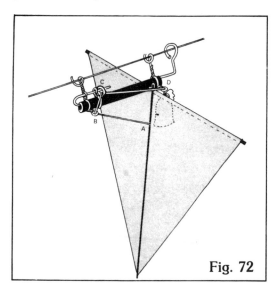

Fig. 72

Unfurling of Parachutes

You can make a parachute launcher like a pilot—the parachute takes the place of a sail. Hold the parachute in place with a loop of string which is released at the moment of launching. This device cannot function unless the wind is strong enough to inflate the parachute from its departure. In order to help the wind get a better hold on the parachute, you can construct a system that holds the parachute in two places. You can also keep the parachute open by placing a very thin, lightweight rattan circle inside it. Fig. 73 shows both of these possibilities.

Whether the parachute is made from

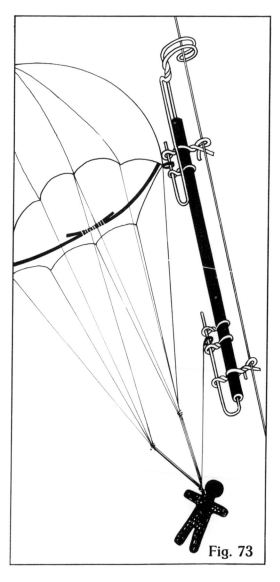

Fig. 73

light fabric or from rice paper, you must assemble it in sections. Cut out a template from newspaper which will be used as a pattern for the sections. Be sure to leave a small opening at the top of the parachute from which the air can escape.

If the body of your parachute is made from paper, the points at which the suspension cords are attached must be reinforced. To prevent these strings from tangling, pass them through a small cardboard circle that keeps them separate (see Fig. 74). You can also group the strings into clusters of four or five, as is done on real parachutes.

Ideas to Explore

Unfurling Pockets

You can make an unfurling pocket from a square of almost any fabric. Attach one corner to the pilot, as shown at 6 in Fig. 75.

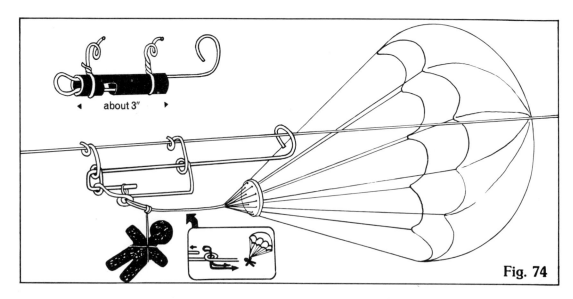

about 3″

Fig. 74

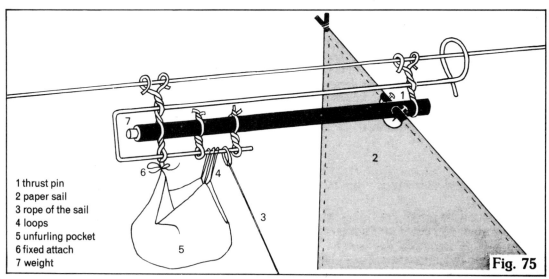

1 thrust pin
2 paper sail
3 rope of the sail
4 loops
5 unfurling pocket
6 fixed attach
7 weight

Fig. 75

Fig. 76

Join the other three corners and attach them at 4 with three separate loops as shown. Let these loops loose at the same time as the rope of the sail.

This pocket can contain a number of different items—for example, small colorful flags that set off a brilliant show of color to liven up a local festival. The pocket can also serve to scatter a message in the wind during a big tournament or rally.

The pocket can also contain an advertising streamer, weighted with bars of wood or sacks of sand. Parachutes can be placed in the pocket that is then released at a high altitude and after which teams can race. The pocket can also contain a surprise treasure. Fig. 76 shows some different ways in which you can use your pocket.

Flying Saucers

You can make one of these flying saucers quite easily. Roll a cone from paper (notebook paper is fine), and pin it together so that it does not unroll. Notch the top edge and fold it down (Fig. 77).

To launch your saucer, first weight the point of the cone with a small stone and let it go into space. The saucer turns as it descends. Several cones made of metallic paper can be released at the same time from the top of the kite.

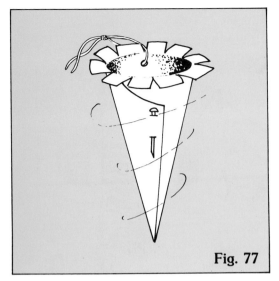

Fig. 77

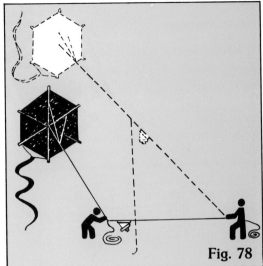

Fig. 78

The Big Shield

A kite can hoist a large shield in honor of a special celebration. You can hang the shield from weighted ropes which are hooked onto the kite's flying line. You can also use a pulley on the flying line to "send the colors" into the open sky. The effect is fantastic, especially if the kite is already far up; the line is made of nylon and the rope carrying the colors is thick and very visible (see Fig. 76).

Aerial Photography

A system of suspension that offers the maximum security for your camera, which also allows it to remain in one direction and under the desired angle, is a necessary element in aerial photography. To help you get started, refer to Figs. 78–80.

One model that we used that gave us good results had a delayed trigger. Once the kite was way up in the air and well supported on a steady air current, we made a quick tug, on the flying line to suspend the gear there (see Fig. 78). Then, as quickly as possible, we let out the line so

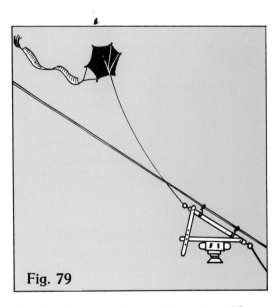

Fig. 79

that the photographic equipment could reach the desired point before shooting.

Meteorological Probings

A team of meteorologists can make some very interesting observations by raising special instruments into the air through the use of a kite; the instruments permit them to take the temperature, to measure the altitude or to calculate the speed of the wind.

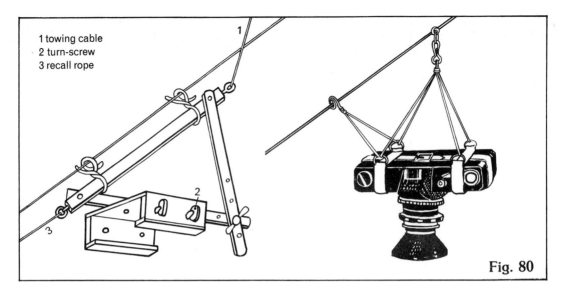

Fig. 80

Why not try to attach a simple strip of sticky "fly paper" to your kite, and send it into the air? When you pull your kite in, you might discover many things if you study the fly paper under a microscope. The air is full of tiny organisms invisible to the naked eye.

As you can see, if you are interested, you can do quite a bit of scientific experimentation using your kite.

Aerial Traction

We have already discussed some experiments done in this area. If you have a kayak or a canoe, what fun to have it pulled by a kite!

If you do not own a boat, you can cut out a small model boat from a piece of thick wood (see Fig. 81). You can launch one boat or even an entire fleet of such models to be towed in a river. If you use your imagination, you can see that this can be the source of innumerable games, including racing.

If a single boat is not heavy enough to offer the proper resistance to the wind, make an entire flotilla for your kite to haul. If you arrange a race, it might also be interesting to transfer provisions (fishing gear, for example) for the teams to a raft.

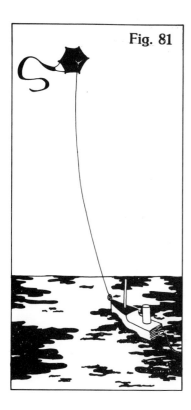

Fig. 81

A Train of Kites

Among the different uses of kites that we have discussed so far, certain ones necessitate increasing strength or fairly considerable traction. In such instances, you can harness together as many kites as necessary. There are two methods for doing this: harnessing "in file" or end-to-end, and harnessing "in a chain."

In the first type, hook the kites to each other, at a distance that you can adjust. The Chinese dragon (see page 56) or Baden-Powell's kite (see page 44) are good illustrations of this type of kite. Making this kind of harness requires that the supports be proportionate in length to the force they will furnish. Their pulling can be eased by carefully placing the attachment point on each element at the place that would be its extension on the next piece.

For the second type of harnessing de-vice, attach the kites by annex cables to a single flying line. To do this, launch a first kite and, just at the point that it finds sufficient stability, let out the line. At this point, another kite should be sent up. When this kite is well up in the air, attach it to the first line that was let out. Begin this operation again with additional kites. An example of this creation is shown in Fig. 76. Generally, it is this type of train that kite flyers use to reach long distances or to break altitude records.

It goes without saying that the more weight you plan to pull with your device, the stronger the traction must be; therefore, the weight must be taken into consideration when a material for the flying line is chosen.

Calculating the Altitude

If your kite is flying over a horizontal area, estimating its altitude using a triangle is very simple. Follow the drawings shown in Fig. 83. First fold a square of heavy paper in two, along the diagonal. Thread a weighted string along one of the small sides as shown. Holding this device at eye level, walk forward or backwards just until you see the flying kite at the elongation of the diagonal of the paper triangle. At the same time, ask a helper to stand with a straight stick as exactly perpendicular to the kite as possible. You should now make a new sighting, but this time by the horizontal side of the triangle. Ask your helper to slide a hand along the stick until it reaches your eye level. The distance between you and your helper, added to the height marked on the stick, gives you the altitude of your kite. If the kite is very high up, the error in evaluation makes the height of the stick of negligible importance.

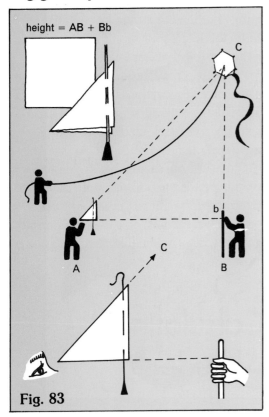

height = AB + Bb

Fig. 83

Noisemaker Kites

Far Easterners used to equip their kites with all sorts of instruments capable of emitting both harmonious and discordant sounds; these included vibrating plates, whistles and kazoos. You read that this practice was transmitted to the Soviet Union in the form of paper vibrators, and Jobert used this idea for his rescue kite, equipped with vibrating blades that struck loudly against each other.

Now it is your turn to make some discoveries in this area. To imitate the principle of the *ek* (a type of arch, as used in the Vietnamese kites, across which is stretched a thin blade of bamboo), use elastic bands to stretch a strip of foil across a bow-shaped frame.

You can also create a type of harp by superimposing different-sized blades, one on top of the other, that you separate with wedges. The hardest thing is to find the position in which to place the blades so that they face correctly into the wind. The same problem exists if you wish to attach a whistle or flute to your kite.

To make a birdcall whistle, stretch a piece of paper tape, as shown in Fig. 84, between two thin strips of wood. A strip of

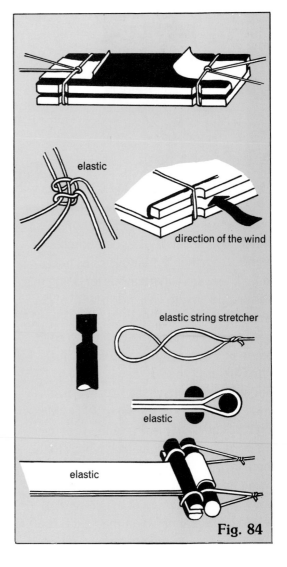

elastic

direction of the wind

elastic string stretcher

elastic

elastic

Fig. 84

tissue paper, neatly cut, stretched between two pieces of cardboard or construction paper to produce pleasant "music" can also be used. A wide and thin rubber bracelet, folded over and stretched tightly, results in harmonious melodies when the wind vibrates the surfaces (see Fig. 84).

The Vietnamese also make a type of kazoo with a piece of bamboo ended by two knots, into whose ends they cut slits about an inch (several millimetres) wide.

Sparrow-Hawk Kite with Rudder

After you have constructed a paper kite, here is an amusing improvement that you can make: Add some wings and a revolving tail that allow your kite to fly at a great height.

In Fig. 85-1, consider the two sticks B

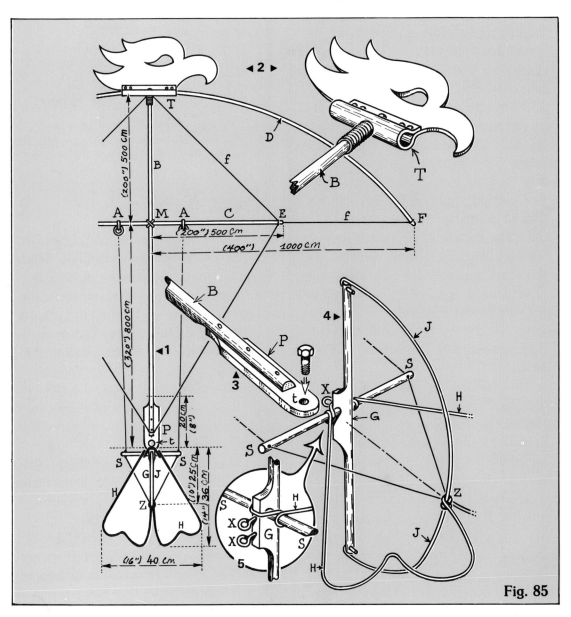

Fig. 85

and C that cross at M. At the top, cut out a predator's head like the one shown from a piece of extra-thin aluminum (from a pie tin, for example). Roll the end as shown in Fig. 85-2, in order to form a tube T, which is fastened in place with several bolts. Screw this entire piece at the end of B, reinforcing the joint by tying it with fine string. At the bottom of the kite, B ends with a palette-shaped piece of wood. Drill a hole in the very end of P (see Fig. 85-3).

Essentially, the fins shown in Fig. 85-4 consist of two pieces of wood: G, a small plank that is shaped into a rounded stick at both ends, and SS, a rounded stick that fits together with G in a cross. Fasten a half-circle of lightweight aluminum wire J to G.

Attach another piece of aluminum wire H to SS. The two ends of H meet at Z after a complicated circuit, which is shown in Fig. 85-1.

Cover this entire construction with paper, as you did for the kite itself. To complete the kite, make a sort of arc forming wings. Fit together two thin, flexible stems opposite each other inside tube T, and use string to stretch between E and F. Notice in Fig. 85-1 that stick C has two rings A and A that are carefully tied and spaced about 8 to 10 inches (20 to 25 cm) apart.

Now fasten two screw eyes X and X on the fins. Place them exactly as far apart as the thickness of the plank P (see Fig. 85-3 and 85-5). Using a small bicycle bolt, assemble X with P. Adjust the connection so that it is tight.

Use two strings instead of one to launch this kite. Pass each one of the strings through a ring A and attach it to one end of S (see Fig. 86). Use a double winder with a wooden string-holding device in the middle, as shown. When the kite is up high,

activate the rudder by pulling sharply on one of the two lines. Equilibrium of the kite can be ensured by placing a small bag of weights along B.

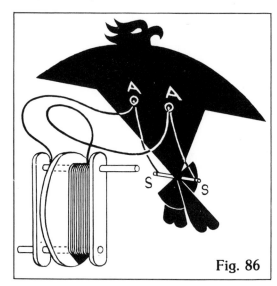

Fig. 86

Box Kite

For the wooden parts of this type of kite, the best material to use is bamboo, which you slit lengthwise and then polish with a knife and sandpaper. You can also use a hard wood or cane. The best string to use is fishing line. Make the sail from heavy paper which can be reinforced along the edges by adding a hem into which you thread a stiff string. You can also make the sail from silk pongee or another lightweight but strong fabric, strengthened with a light coat of varnish.

Fig. 87 shows the completed kite. Notice that all the sides are indicated in the drawing. Be sure that the two cells are connected first on the corner sticks.

Fig. 88-1 shows the diagram of one of the four sides to which two wing flaps are attached. Note the two stretched support ropes knotted together at their crossing

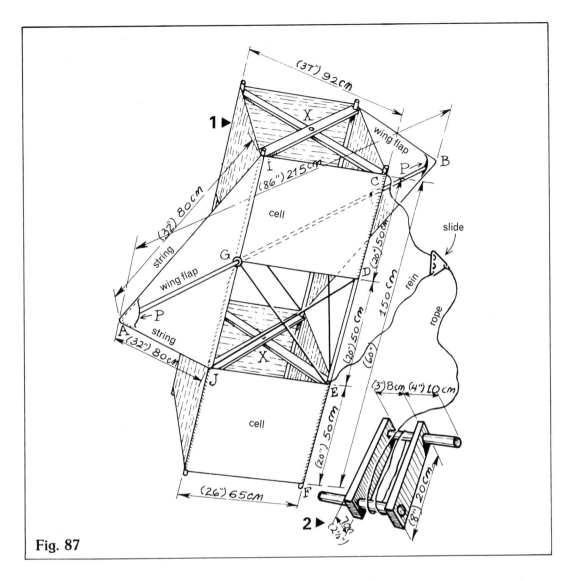

Fig. 87

that are in the space between the two cells.

Sew the wing flap between I and J. Firmly attach a large ring—you can use a large copper curtain ring—at G.

Stretch the two wing flaps along a long stick AB, which you pass through ring G and then fit into two small triangular pockets P at the ends. Stick AB can be curved gently so that it fits correctly.

To maintain the rigidity of the kite, four wooden "X's" are to be wedged inside the cells at points C, D, and E and F; Fig. 88-3 shows the details of one of these X's. The

X is formed from two narrow strips of wood (H) held together by a small bolt and two washers. Note that the X that is placed at point D, however, is different: It consists of only one strip of wood (see Fig. 88-4). The other strip is replaced by stick AB. Notice that AB is detachable into two separate pieces which are assembled together into an aluminum casing M that is tied firmly to H.

Fig. 88-5 shows one of the points of the wedging of the H sticks on the side sticks of the kite itself, between two whips of fine

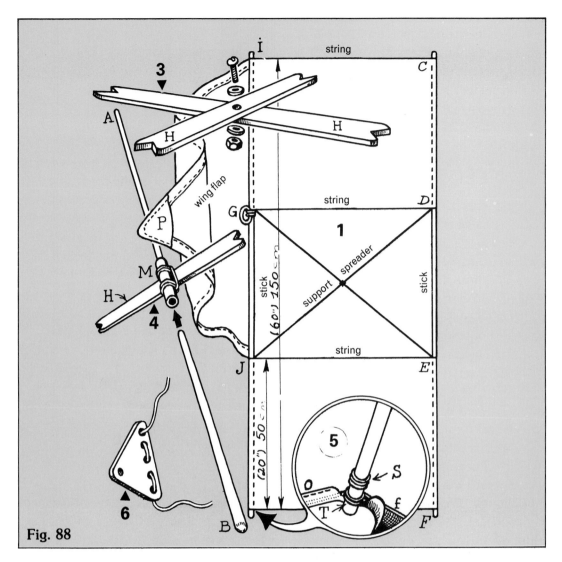

Fig. 88

string S and T, which prevent the sticks from slipping. Fig. 88-5 shows how the cell is sewn around the string that surrounds it.

Attach a bridle about 1½ yards (1.5 metres) long at C and E (see Fig. 87). Place a special triangular slide made from a thin piece of wood (drilled with five holes along this bridle), as shown in the drawing. This slide allows you to regulate the pulling of the cord; you can determine the exact location of the slide by trial-and-error attempts at flying the kite. The upper branch of the cord should be shorter than the bottom branch.

Complete this kite by making a wooden reel, shown in Fig. 87-2, to hold the cord.

Signalling by Kite

To produce daytime or nighttime signals with your kite, an altitude of 200 to 500 yards (200 to 500 metres) is sufficient. The position on the cord from which you launch your signals must be located about 40 to 50 yards (40 to 50 metres) underneath the kite itself. You cannot successfully release any signals until your kite has reached enough height to ensure its carrying strength. There are many ways you can create a successful signal system; two methods—daytime and nighttime signals—are described below.

Daytime Signals

This kite consists of a thrust block and a post. The block (see Fig. 89-1) is a small wooden ruler, U, which is attached to the cord of the kite about 40 or 50 yards (40 or 50 metres) from the glider by means of two small metal loops. Keep this wooden piece U above the cord by suspending a counterweight P under it, using a piece of metal wire. In a slit you cut in the bottom edge of the block, insert a razor blade L, as shown in Fig. 89-1. This blade must not cross the cord; it is essential that it be very slanted in relation to the cord.

The post is a long, squared wooden rod, R, which slides along the cord with the help of two porcelain insulators, I and I (see Fig. 89-2). Attach a piece of tin cut out as shown in Fig. 89-3 (piece F) to the front of the post. Also at this point, attach a lightweight, tapered wooden rod AB to which triangular sail V is fastened. Determine the proper size for V through trial and error.

Hang a cockpit N from the wooden rod R at point E using cords S. Make this box-shaped cockpit from a lightweight material. The hinged lid belongs on the bottom. Close it by a catch O, held taut by a piece of fine thread W, which is knotted at F. Fig. 89-4 shows the vertical cross section of the cockpit N. The signals D—which are described in more detail later—are folded inside the box. They are attached to a cord kept in a Z-shape. This cord forms a loop G that immobilizes the sheet (special rope)

that holds the sail, which enters into the box by the hole T (see Figs. 89-2 and 89-4). The other end of the cord ends with a suspended weight M.

Functioning

When the kite reaches the desired height, carrying along with it the abutment, place the main post on the cord using the two isolators I. The cockpit contains the desired signals. The wind inflates the sail V, which carries with it the assembly along the cord. The main post collides with the block, the string W opens the bottom of the cockpit N and the signals, led by the weight M, fall and spread out. This drop provokes a strong pulling against loop G. The sheet of the sail frees itself, and the sail is no longer held stretched out. The main post redescends along the cord, while the onlookers observe the signal being sent. The main post can be launched a second time with a new set of signals.

Signals

Fig. 89-5 shows two different types of signals. The ones on the right are flags made from lightweight fabric, which can be made to correspond to an agreed-upon code. The flags on the left are cut from black material. They are stretched between sticks and assembled lengthwise to compose letters in Morse code. These are read from top to bottom.

Determine the size of the long cord that holds the signals by several tries from the ground. The weight of the cord must be sufficient to hold the code down towards the ground.

Nighttime Signals

You can send bright signals by using a

main post that lifts up different-colored paper lanterns. However, for an even more brilliant arrangement, follow these directions for making a system that functions by battery:

Refer to Fig. 90-1 as you work. To begin, you need two wooden discs, D_1 and D_2, each of which carries a long loop made from rigid wire. Loop E_1 forms ring A, which you attach to disc D_1. E_1 slides freely across D_2 through holes a and a. Likewise, loop E_2 forms ring B, which you attach to disc D_2; it slides freely across D_1 through holes b and b. The middle of disc D_1 contains a not-too-strong electric bulb P which is straddled by a very small loop C.

A thick elastic swivel, L_1, pulls disc D_2 towards A; T_1 is set between a strong screw eye and ring A. Likewise, disc D_1 is pulled towards B by a swivel L_2. T_2 is set between rings B and C. The pulling of each side should balance the other.

Wedge this entire assembly on the cord of the kite, about 40 yards (40 metres)

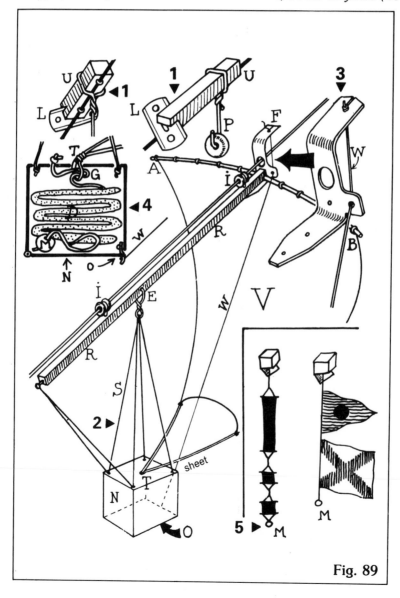

Fig. 89

below the kite. Cut the kite's cord and attach the two resulting ends to loops A and B using snap hooks.

Hang a large white disc R about one yard (one metre) above the assembly. Attach an electric lamp to this disc. On top of the plateau of the disc, as shown in Fig. 90-2, fit a casing for the battery H. You can, for example, tighten the battery between two corner brackets, G, using a strip of rubber, S. The flexible wire F, coming from the bulb P, is attached at Y and Z. Fig. 90-3 shows a cross section of this arrangement. Fig. 90-4 illustrates the mounting of the entire assembly on the kite's cord.

Functioning

Regulate the tension of the swivels T_1 and T_2 so that the pull of the kite in flight puts the switch of the bulb almost in contact with disc D_2. A sharp pull on the cord activates this button and lights up the bulb; the bulb is put out in the same way. In this manner, it is easy to send visible messages to faraway observers on a clear night. It is useless to send this type of arrangement higher than 150 yards (150 metres), unless the terrain is very uneven.

To improve visibility from a great distance, several batteries can be mounted on a plateau that has two or three lamps.

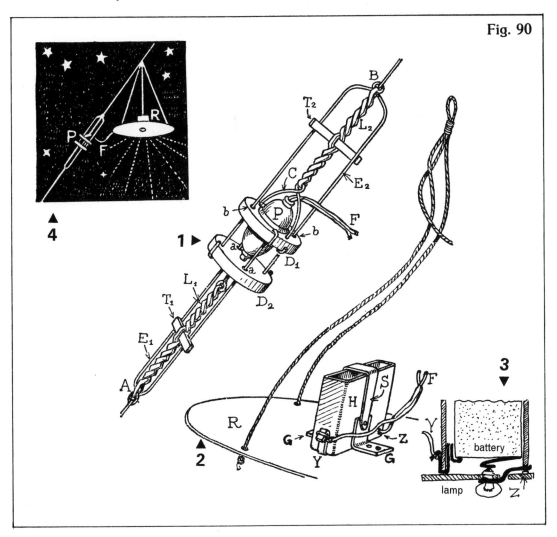

Fig. 90

BEACH TOYS

We begin here by making a simple beach plane and then continue with models that demand more perseverance and skill.

Sand Crabs

The "sand crab" is a toy which is simple to make, and it uses the wind to propel it into motion. The toy, modelled after the movements of a sand crab, works best at a beach or on a windy and flat semi-smooth surface.

A beautiful feather, as well as two long, flexible sticks, is driven into a piece of lightweight cork. In this way, you can obtain a sort of "tripede" whose ends rest lightly on the ground. On a day when there is a good wind, the "crab" is placed on the beach and the feather, acting like a sail, carries it away, zigzagging on its long, flexible legs.

Children can race these sand-crab toys or use them in slaloms, with obligatory passages through certain spots. The penalty for skipping a spot can be to begin again ten steps behind it.

Hoops through which the opponents must pass and spring-boards from which the crabs must jump can be constructed; penalties can be assigned if the toys do not land squarely on two feet, and so on. Also consider adding improvements to your "crabs" to make them more efficient: propellors, rudders, a complementary sail?

The Travois with Rollers or Beach Travois

In modifying the sand-crab toy just described, you might easily arrive at an arrangement that eliminates the feather and replaces it with rollers, necessitating the use of a new type of sail. From there, it is just a short step until you invent a travois (a type of primitive cart) with rollers.

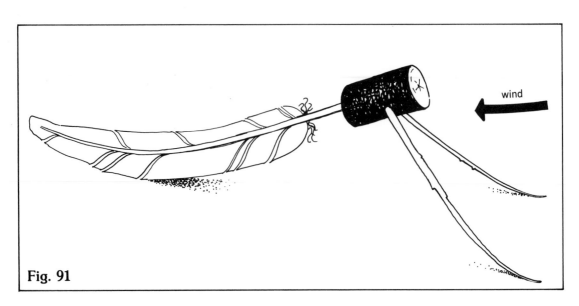

wind

Fig. 91

Here is how to make the travois shown in Fig. 92. Push a stick lengthwise through a piece of cork so that the stick can serve as an axle for two spools that are placed one on either side of the cork. Bolt the axle in place, using a pin on each side; these pins prevent the axle from detaching itself (see Fig. 92). Push two long twigs, as you did for the sand crab, into the cork. These twigs stand and drag along the ground like the poles of an Indian travois. Next, stick a mast—on which you have threaded a pa-per sail—into the cork. All that remains is for you to find some flat clear ground and wait until the breeze comes to do its part!

Some of the same games that can be played using the sand crab can also apply to this little toy; use your imagination to develop others.

Baby Beach Plane

If you attach a third wheel to the previous project, you will diminish the friction of the toy against the ground, thus improving the plane's speed. Fig. 93 (p. 84) shows some ways of doing this.

Add a cross axle through a third spool and connect this arrangement to the two poles of the travois, and you have invented a beach plane! Spools can be used for wheels, or you can use the covers from wooden cheeseboxes or even empty shoe-polish tins for the plane's body. You can make simple sails or more complicated ones—even double ones. Fig. 94 shows another type of plane body you can make with a matchbox, into which you glue a cork. Stick a crossbeam, an axle and a mast right into the cork as shown.

Here again, you have the opportunity to make many different creations if you use your imagination.

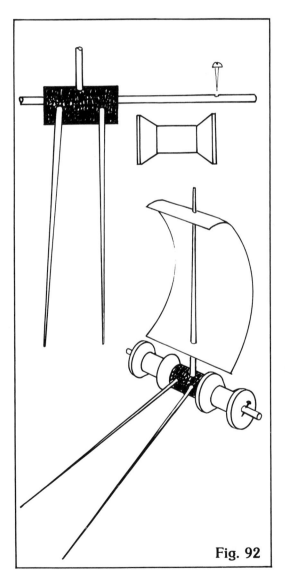

Fig. 92

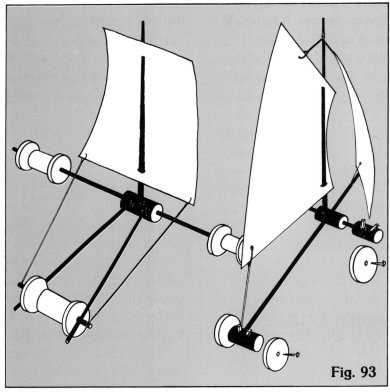

Fig. 93

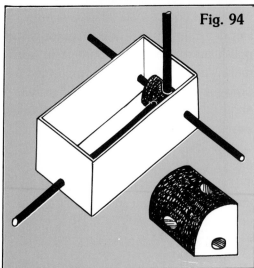

Fig. 94

The Great Sport Beach Plane

Now you are ready to abandon the cork, spools and paper to work with more substantial materials. It is up to you to decide what type of material to use. Cut the fabric with the grain and leave an extra margin for the hem when you sew the sails.

Your first attempts are actually a trial-and-error process, but you will discover rather quickly that one of the conditions for making a successful beach plane is that it be as stable as possible so that it does not capsize or make brisk head-to-tail spins with a sharp blast of wind. Such inconveniences can be avoided by pasting a float on the front and by making the hull sufficiently long. The correct dimensions will be arrived at with practice, because many elements must be taken into consideration: the weight of the wood and the height, surface and shape of the sail of your vessel, for example. In addition, if the hull is heavy, you might want to move the location of the mast towards the bow to relieve the back wheel. Or, on the other hand, if your little boat is very light, the mast can be planted so that it is perpendicular to the axle of the wheels. This reduces the risk of the boat's falling on its nose. A system of weights can be arranged by constructing a small box that is harnessed to the rear, as shown in Fig. 95. This also helps to balance the boat.

Large sails—a yard (one metre) or more in height—can be made with this type of construction. Rigging for such a vessel can resemble the rigging of a real boat: pulleys, belaying pins for the ropes and reefs for the sails (see the bottom left-hand corner of Fig. 95).

To make an even more substantial boat, refer to a good marine guidebook.

One of the difficulties in making such planes is ensuring the roundness of the wheels. You can saw them out from a wooden plank, but you must be sure they are perfectly rounded. Wheels can be made by connecting two covers from round metal boxes, as from shoe polish, one against the other. To do this, determine the middle of the cover so that you can pierce a hole there through which you pass a screw serving as the axle. The middle of the metal lid can be determined easily. Trace the outline of the lid onto a piece of paper; cut out the circle and then fold it in four. The intersection of the folds gives the exact middle point; place the template on the metal lid and mark the placement of the middle. Cut out the axle's hole. To join the two halves of the wheel, place a wedge between them that is thick enough to fill in the space between the halves when you put them edge to edge. You can use a spool to fill in this space.

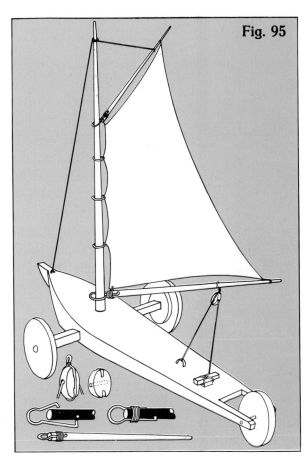

Fig. 95

WIND MACHINES

Trailers

A row of trailers can be attached to a beach plane that contributes to its stability when the wind is very strong. Here again, you have a choice of what type of trailer to adopt. Choose between a three- or four-wheeled model (see Fig. 96). Go to a train station and study the cars and how they are connected.

Arabian Pinwheel

This small four-winged pinwheel is made from palm leaves; follow Fig. 97 to create yours.

To begin, two thongs made from cattail leaves (or from any two stiff weeds) are needed. One serves as a base; begin with the other as shown in Fig. 97-1. Surround the base strand two or three times with the other, as shown in Fig. 97-2. Fold back the thong at a 45-degree angle, and pass the end under its own rollings (Fig. 97-3); tighten. Pull out the base thong to obtain a thong ended in a loop like that on a belt. Begin the operation again with another thong (Fig. 97-4). Do the same for another pair. Thread the ends of the two knots on

each base into each other, as shown in Fig. 97-5, but before the ends are tightened, wedge one pair into the other in order to form a cross as shown. Pierce the middle of the pinwheel with a sharp pin. Holding the pin, run with your pinwheel or face the wind to see it whirl.

Monoplane Propellor

You can make charming little airplanes using some branches that are cut and assembled. Follow the steps shown in Fig. 98. An airfield equipped with "lights" made from the red berries from a local shrub can be made for the airplane, along with an airshaft made from a rolled-up leaf and a control tower made from an empty cardboard tube or other similar material.

Propellor with a String Motor

Make a propellor from a piece of wood in the middle of which you pierce two

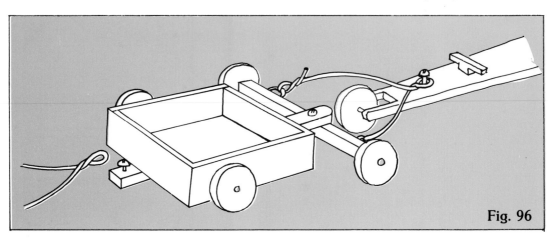

Fig. 96

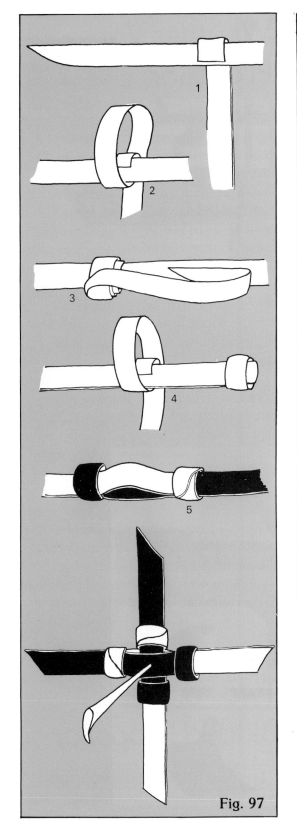

Fig. 97

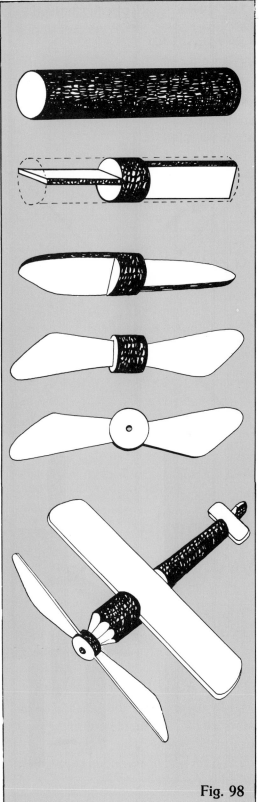

Fig. 98

holes. Thread a piece of string through these holes. Make a small, inconspicuous knot. Twist the string, as shown in Fig. 99, and pull abruptly on its ends. Bring your hands towards each other in order to begin the procedure again. This has the effect of turning the propellor first in one direction, then in the other.

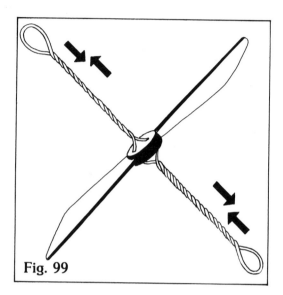

Fig. 99

A Simple Weather Vane

You can now make a propellor that is practical: a weather vane. This little gadget can also be used in place of a scarecrow in your garden.

Follow Fig. 100. From a branch cut a propellor big enough to be attached to the end of another branch that forms the main body of the weather vane. Cut out a rudder from a lid of a wooden cheese box and drive it in to the opposite end, as shown.

Weather Vane-Propellor

The scarecrow shown in the photograph on page 92 was coarsely carved out of balsa wood; a log or rafter can be used to carve a similar figure. Mount the body on a swivel placed at the end of a stake that has been pushed into the ground. Make the arms from two blades of a wooden propellor. Pass a piece of wire (which serves as an axle) through the body to interconnect the two arms. When the wind blows, the arms begin to turn, and the scarecrow agitates about, in all directions, thus chasing away unwelcome birds from your garden.

Instead of a scarecrow, you can use the construction techniques to create an athlete swinging his or her arms or a police officer conducting heavy traffic with two batons. Why not create a bird flapping its wings?

All the weather vanes discussed so far have been made of wood, but there is no reason why you cannot experiment with cardboard instead. To obtain the slant of the propellor's blades against the body, cut wedges from a piece of cork and glue them to the cardboard.

Two- or Four-Bladed Propellor

In making this type of propellor, temporarily abandon the type of weather vane that turns freely on an axle and consider

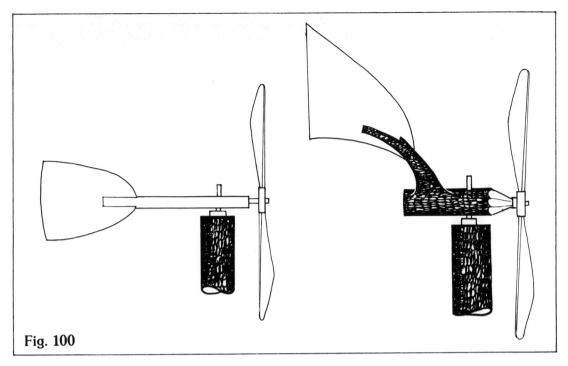

Fig. 100

instead a windmill whose axle activates something.

The propellor shown in Fig. 101 is mounted on a pivoting chassis and is equipped with a rudder. Carefully cut out the boss (the raised part for the propellor) in a piece of balsa wood so that the hole for the axle is exactly in the middle and the two arms balance perfectly. Bevel the edges of the arms in the opposite directions (as shown in Fig. 101), to an angle of about 25 degrees. The direction of the bevelling determines the direction of the rotation, a fact which is particularly important to keep in mind if you are creating a device with two propellors that move in opposite directions.

Cut out the two blades from a thin piece

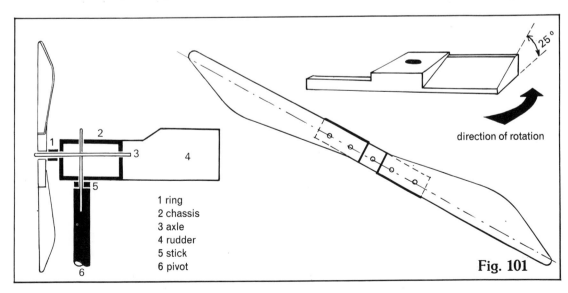

direction of rotation

1 ring
2 chassis
3 axle
4 rudder
5 stick
6 pivot

Fig. 101

of balsa wood, lightweight metal or a piece of acrylic. If you plan to keep your project sheltered from the rain, you can even make the blades from cardboard. Glue them and then screw them onto the arms of the boss you previously cut out. Use a nail, screw or bolt to hold the axle immobilized in the hole in the boss.

To reduce the rubbing and to facilitate the rotation, thread a ring onto the axle (between the propellor and the chassis). Once the propellor is mounted, it will turn in even the slightest wind and will be able to stop in any position if it is well balanced. You can attach a counterweight (a piece of metal or a marble) to the end of the boss's arm, on the side that is too light.

This method of construction allows you to make very large propellors with impressive drive forces.

To create an even more powerful device, you can make two simple propellors and fit their bosses one inside the other as shown in Fig. 102. In this way, you end up with a four-winged propellor.

Musical Mill

The parts your finished music box should have are shown in Fig. 103. Build a

wooden box as shown. Drill holes for the axle and insert it through the box from side to side. After the axle is in place, attach two leather thongs to it that each hold up a metal ring. The axle must be able to move freely after the thongs and rings are attached. Hang a copper plaque or tube from the side of the chassis, as shown in Fig. 103. When you turn the axle, the rings gently clang against the copper. Fig. 104 shows the position of the propellor at the end of the axle.

The quality of the sound your device

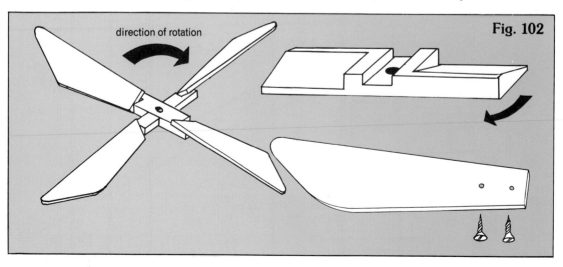

direction of rotation

Fig. 102

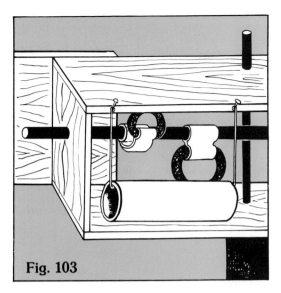

Fig. 103

produces can be regulated by carefully choosing the thickness and number of the copper plaques or tubes.

Drum Mill

Make the basic body of this mill in the same way as for the musical mill just described (see Fig. 104), except that you attach a drum. The drum can be made from a hollowed-out log on which you stretch a piece of hide. In place of hide, you can also use a piece of fabric, but the sound you produce in this way is not as clear.

You can hang one or more drums on the side of the box. After you do this, mount a series of drumsticks held in place by special spacers (see Fig. 104-3) on an axle inserted for this purpose. Make the head of each drumstick by rolling string or pieces of elastic cut from an old inner tube around a stick. Cover this with a piece of leather or fabric, and nail blades as shown in Fig. 104-1 to the propellor's axle. In adjusting the blades to the proper position, be sure to consider the direction of the rotation of the propellor so that the blades are not pulled out or blocking the mill. If you calculate well, your drum will produce an authentic drum beat.

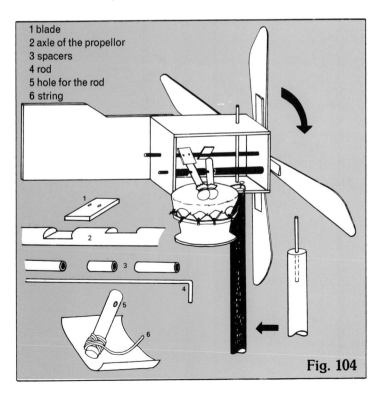

1 blade
2 axle of the propellor
3 spacers
4 rod
5 hole for the rod
6 string

Fig. 104

Vibrating Mill

Have you ever heard of a *sanza* or *m'bichi*? It is a resonance box cut out from a piece of wood on which are attached metal strips or not-too-thick bamboo blades and which rest under small crossbars (see Fig. 105). The art involved is to make the blades vibrate in cadence to accompany a song. It is easy to adapt this instrument for use with a mill. Hammer a series of nails into the axle of the propellor. These form spurs that make the bamboo or metal blades you attached to the resonance box vibrate (see Fig. 105).

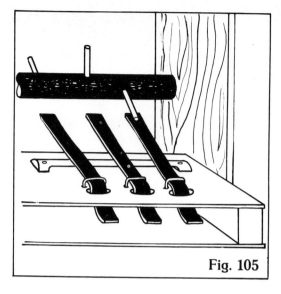

Fig. 105

Little Devil Mill

Here, top the chassis of your mill with a sort of box from which alternating colored little devils pop. Mount each devil on a stem that contains a sector (a portion of a circle) and which moves in and out of specially notched slides (see Fig. 106-2). Place control levers at different positions along the axle of the propellor; these serve to raise and lower the devils in turn as the axle rotates. Be careful to consider where to place these levers to control the rotation so that they take the sectors from underneath to raise them up and not block them from below.

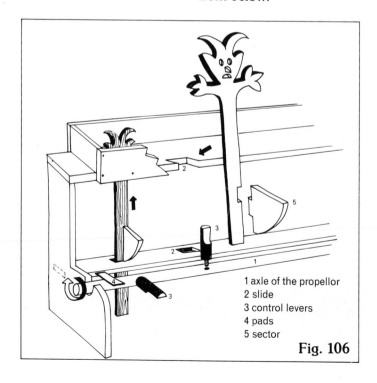

1 axle of the propellor
2 slide
3 control levers
4 pads
5 sector

Fig. 106

Automaton Mill

It goes without saying that your mill can animate all sorts of objects, such as wooden people and animals, by utilizing either a small cam placed at the end of the axle or a system of repeats, transmissions and cranks (Figs. 107–110).

In calculating a new model, always consider the direction in which the transmission axle rotates. Realize what happens in the case of a return in the back if, because of a drop in the wind, a blade of the propellor falls before finishing its course; the arms of the levers for the fisherman or boxers must be long enough so that the cam cannot lift them from the end.

Other problems might also arise. For the fisherman in Fig. 109, it is necessary to include a stopper by either hammering in a nail behind the arms of the lever or by placing a small shelf under the feet. In Fig. 110, the bottom of the counterweight must rest a little above the axle of the cam in order to ensure good movement.

Fig. 107

Fig. 109

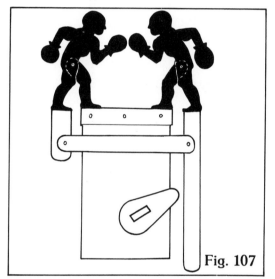

Fig. 108

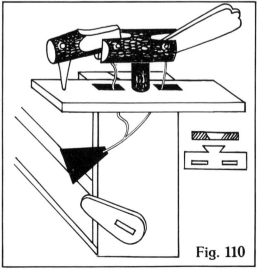

Fig. 110

Index